Education and
Social Action

Education and Social Action

Community Service and the Curriculum
in Higher Education

EDITED BY SINCLAIR GOODLAD
Imperial College, University of London

BOOKS
10 East 53d St., New York 10022
(a division of Harper & Row Publishers, Inc.)

Published in the U.S.A. 1975 by
Harper & Row, Publishers, Inc
Barnes & Noble Import Division

ISBN 0-06-492485-8

Printed in Great Britain

Foreword

BY ALEC DICKSON, C.B.E., LL.D.,
Founder of Voluntary Service Overseas,
Honorary Director and Founder of Community Service Volunteers

At the University of Hacettepe, on the outskirts of Ankara, students registering for the medical school are assigned responsibility for the health of a Turkish family living in a slum area of the city. Throughout their years of study they act as 'medical friend' of the family – and in this they have, naturally, the backing of the faculty. When they ultimately receive their degree, much of their knowledge of community medicine has not been learnt from books or lectures: it has been acquired at first hand. Moreover, the development of a sense of social responsibility towards the sick has not been left to chance: it has been built into their course of study from the very first day.

Farmers on the slopes of Mount Merapi in Central Java, despite the volcanic eruptions which, from time to time, used to destroy their crops and endanger their homes, rejected offers from officials to resettle them elsewhere, being suspicious of the Government's motives and strongly attached to their land. Whereupon the faculty of social and political science at the nearby University of Gadja Maja intervened. Carefully analysing the arguments that would carry weight with the peasants (and yet be genuinely in their interest), and concluding that the decision whether or not a family should move was made by the women, the faculty sent in their girl students – and the peasants agreed to be resettled. Study or service? Manifestly a combination of both.

Intentionally, it is from the Third World that I have quoted these examples of the curricular approach to the involvement of students in community service. Partly because the very intensity of the problems facing these countries is compelling the more perceptive university authorities to enable their students to apply their skills and knowledge to national needs as an integral part of their courses. Partly because in a less sophisticated society certain truths are more clearly discernible – notably that when the umbilical cord between learning and doing is severed, processes are set in train which can lead to tragic consequences. The Asian girl learning to reap as she harvests, the African boy adding to the catch as he learns to fish, give way to thousands of unemployed B.A.s whose study has never merged with any form of action and today bears virtually no relevance to the community's needs. There must be, one senses, something so elemental and valid about this basic concept of apprenticeship – that in creating one learns, and in learning creates – that we abandon it at our peril.

The assumption hitherto has been that only after mastering a subject, only after completion of studies, is the individual entitled or competent to practise his skills. Against this belief we juxtapose the conviction that the very process of acquiring knowledge can contribute to human needs. The act of learning can itself be of help to others.

Until now 'service' has been seen as a separate entity, either quite distinct from study, or – if included in the curriculum – a special subject in its own right. The imperfections of both approaches have been very evident in secondary education. When helping is viewed as a hobby, outside the mainstream of education on the one hand or of urgent human needs on the other, inevitably the concept of service itself and the nature of the tasks undertaken assume only peripheral significance. And so the few who are drawn, by family background or personal inclination, to participate in what are listed as leisure-time activities (or, in some schools still, as alternatives to games or the cadet force) remain a small minority group. What they do lacks, both intellectually and socially, a cutting edge.

Nor is any provision made for an element of growth in this extra-curricular approach. At thirteen, as likely as not, they visit the elderly; at fifteen they do still; and at seventeen or eighteen – in diminishing numbers – they undertake the same form of service. In effect, they are all stuck at book one: they have not progressed – as they would have done in any other school activity – to more demanding tasks, commensurate with their mental and physical development. By continual small doses of the same, many become inoculated against the possibility of a major 'take': an immunity has been built up against a wider understanding of social problems or a desire for deeper involvement.

But unfortunately when a place is found in the timetable for Community Service as a subject in its *own* right – whether under that name or as civics, moral education or general studies – the results are not all that encouraging. In the hundreds of schools which have adopted this approach, since two small paragraphs in the Newsom Report of ten years ago advocated the involvement of early leavers in community service projects, this has become the preserve of the least intellectually gifted – as woodwork used to be before the war – indeed, it is looked upon by many as a form of remedial education, as though service was something for the coolies. The academic aspirations of older and abler pupils, on the other hand, are held to exonerate them from participation, with the staff condoning this exemption on account of examination pressures. Sir Alan Bullock, in a vivid phrase, has described the consequences of this approach as guaranteeing the emergence of 'an illegitimate elite'.

Even when curriculum provision is extended to include sixth formers – under the title of social science or modern studies – surveys, observation and analysis predominate at the expense of action to meet a human need. The Humanities Project developed on behalf of the Schools Council, for example, comprises case studies, cuttings and articles brilliantly descriptive of man's predicament today, from starvation in Bihar to immigrant tensions in Birmingham, but then leaves pupils to draw their own conclusions and pass on to the next lesson. By arousing their concern yet stopping on the brink of action – a kind of titillation – the project denies them the benefit of what the Americans call experiential learning, the understanding that derives from actual involvement in the plight of others and the search for solutions to real-life problems.

Yet in all these schools the probability is that science is stimulating both intellectual curiosity and a readiness to act. When the problem under investigation relates to human need, the response can be a wonderful blend of imagination and creativity. The Gateway School in Leicester comes to mind, where pupils have produced complete libraries of tactile maps for the blind, a machine to provide audio-stimuli at various pitches to help with the psychological analysis of autism, adapters to assist arthritic people to handle Yale-type keys and a vehicle to enable children suffering from congenital hip disorder to propel themselves both indoors and out. Or one thinks of Walkden County Secondary School, where fourteen-year-olds have developed an alarm clock to waken the deaf, devised apparatus to alert passers-by if a baby is snatched from a pram and invented a mechanism to warn neighbours should elderly folk, living alone, collapse in their homes. The advantages, both educational and social, of approaching human need as a problem to be solved, whether by science or some other process – in contrast to isolating 'service' as a separate entity, or structuring it as a special subject in its own right – would seem to be over-whelming. It is as though the process of separation sterilises both service and study, resulting in a kind of pasteurised compassion.

Study and service are usually separated in higher education too. Despite the explosive advent of campus unrest, Student Community Action – with its championing of tenants' rights, claimants' unions, welfare rights, environmental conservation, or international issues such as Vietnam, Rhodesia and the Third World – has left the curriculum more or less intact.

The warm-hearted student of bio-chemistry, who devotes his spare time to teaching spastic children to swim, and the militant radical, who challenges the Vice-Chancellor's authority, may seem poles apart: what they share in common is that their concern is, by and large, unrelated to their course of study. And the establish-ment of social action groups in colleges has, in many instances, resulted in deflecting attention from the case for linking the curricu-lum itself to human needs.

The same sense of unfulfilment, felt in schools which have made responsibility for human need a subject in its own right, emerges in colleges that have invested their social concern in departments of sociology. Paradoxically, the sharpening of focus that might be assumed to follow from one particular department concentrating its efforts to this end – as contrasted with the more diffused approach whereby this objective is shared by a multiplicity of faculties – is seldom realised. But, as the chapters of this book show, worth-while links between Community Service and the curriculum can be achieved by faculties not directly concerned with sociology or social work.

The answer to those who stress the neutrality of knowledge is that, whilst the professional academic is free to engage in the disinterested pursuit of truth, the ordinary degree-taking student is not. He does not study a subject, he follows a *course* – a course whose components, references, limits and duration have been pre-determined by an individual or committee.

Certainly the intellectual challenge is sharpened when the stress is on problem solving rather than the study of discovered truths. It stimulates inquiry, reversing the concentration on the analytical at the expense of the creative.

Contents

Contents

Introduction

Community Service and the Curriculum in Higher Education

BY SINCLAIR GOODLAD

Sinclair Goodlad is lecturer in Associated Studies (Communication) at the Imperial College of Science and Technology, University of London. He read English at Cambridge University and took a Ph.D. in Sociology at the London School of Economics. He has lectured in English at St Stephen's College, Delhi University and was visiting lecturer in the Humanities Department at the Massachusetts Institute of Technology before going to Imperial College. He is author of *A Sociology of Popular Drama*, 1971, and *Science for Non-Scientists*, 1973.[1]

BACKGROUND: THE PURPOSE OF THE BOOK

This book examines the possibility and value of effecting links between Community Service and the curriculum in various sectors of higher education. It has three principal aims:

1 To describe what has been done in each of several disciplines in giving students the opportunity to carry out work of direct social utility within the context of the curriculum.
2 To examine the benefits and problems experienced by students, their teachers and those whom they seek to serve in the activities described.
3 To analyse the social and educational issues involved in each activity.

The initiative for the book derives from the current work of Community Service Volunteers in fostering links between Community Service and the curriculum, not only in schools, but also in institutions of higher education. It also reflects the continuing debate about the social relevance of British education, and the independent initiatives of institutions of higher education in attempting to provide some form of Community Service or to become involved in more radical community action.

For several years, the advisory service of Community Service Volunteers has been helping schools to develop their own programmes of Community Service. Experience in this field suggested that there was a strong case for relating Community Service to the *curriculum* – rather than seeing it as something quite separate, beginning only after classroom work had finished, and then often as an alternative to sports or combined cadet force. Community Service Volunteers proposed and prepared Working Paper No. 17 for the Schools Council, on 'Community Service and the Curriculum' (1968),[2] which has made an appreciable impact. More recently, Community Service Volunteers has been receiving a steadily increasing number of requests for advice as to how students pursuing higher education courses can relate their studies to social problems and human needs.

The interest expressed to Community Service Volunteers in this way suggests that there is a need for a book which describes in some detail what has been done where, by whom, for what purpose and with what effect, so that those contemplating a linkage between curriculum and Community Service may know what are the benefits and practical problems involved in any such work. This book seeks to meet that need. In his Foreword, Alec Dickson has expressed forcefully some of the impatience which many social reformers feel at the apparent remoteness from urgent social problems shown by institutions of higher education – in particular, universities. If criticism of the apparent social indolence of universities is to bear fruit in intelligent action, the debate about the social relevance of education must be examined through the detailed study of problems experienced in disciplines where social action has been linked to the curriculum.

This book is not a text book. Nor does it claim to be a comprehensive coverage of all forms of action linking Community Service and the curriculum. However, the activities described in the chapters which follow are ones which represent some years of experience on the part of each of the authors, and which raise social and educational issues which may be generalised to other disciplines and to other social activities. Each chapter is a self-contained study based upon some practical activity, and raising an educational issue of primary relevance in the discipline discussed, but also of more general import. The arrangement of the chapters is reviewed briefly on page 30. This introduction highlights some of the difficult questions involved in linking curriculum and social action. To these questions there can be no final answer, for they are largely political questions. Indeed, different philosophies of education and social action inform the various contributions to this book. The debate about principles and practice to which they form a modest contribution will arise whenever the social function of education is considered. The problems concerning education through social action examined in this introduction are likely to be central in any such debate.

Because problems differ only in detail, not necessarily in principle, between institutions of higher education and the more advanced levels of the secondary sector of education, some of the issues discussed in this book should be relevant to work in schools too. The book should also be of interest and value to people working in the social services or in helping organisations who may regard institutions of higher education as 'resource centres' of untapped potential and who may value some indication of the benefits and problems to be anticipated if these institutions of higher education become involved with social problems. Again, the book should be of value to representatives of the professions whose professional institutions have concern for the methods of professional education and training.

Because this book is aimed at such a diverse readership, a word of justification may be needed for its perhaps rather specialised coverage.

Firstly, the argument in the chapters which follow is conducted primarily in terms of the educational benefits likely to accrue to students. The possibility of linking some form of direct practical service to the curriculum is, for many educators, a revolutionary suggestion. Indeed, the potential linkage of Community Service and the curriculum is academically important precisely because it challenges academic assumptions and helps to clarify them. The emphasis on the academic end of the process is necessary because, if educational innovation does not meet the fundamental requirement of providing *long-term* benefit to students, it will not commend itself to institutions of higher education, and will not, of course, be of ultimate benefit to society.

Secondly, universities are perhaps emphasised at the expense of polytechnics, colleges of education, etc. This too is deliberate. The social commitment of polytechnics is more explicit than that of

B

universities. Indeed, George Brosan (1971, page 102)[3] has written that: 'the logistic development of polytechnics owes all to the failure of university involvement with society.' If it can be shown that links between Community Service and the curriculum effectively meet the objectives of university education, it should be correspondingly easier to show how they meet the objectives of institutions dedicated to identifiable social goals rather than to knowledge 'for its own sake'.

There are other very good reasons why one should concentrate on universities. For better or worse, much of what goes on in schools is determined by the preoccupations of universities. For example, I have attempted to demonstrate elsewhere (Goodlad, 1973)[1] that the organisation of science teaching in universities produces a cascade effect throughout the educational system, which is felt even in the Certificate of Secondary Education. In particular, the entry requirements of universities influence sixth form studies in pattern and content so that even those pupils who do not intend to go to universities are often educated as if they did.

Again, universities are colossally expensive: the education of students in universities currently costs upwards of £1,200 per student per year. The public credibility of universities depends upon their being seen to be doing something which is of recognisable benefit for society. An important benefit of community involvement of the universities, it can be argued, is simply that of letting people know what goes on in them.

Thirdly, a further word is needed to justify the selective choice of disciplines. It is clearly important for the professions to be discussed – in this book, law, urban planning, engineering, and teaching. It is perhaps in the professions that the pressures for the social relevance of knowledge are most acutely felt, for knowledge has to be legitimated not only in the *educational* institutions in which professional education is carried out, but also in the *professional* institutions who grant licences or charters to practise. As is argued later, both educational institutions and professional institutions have a tendency to standardise what is permitted as legitimate knowledge, perhaps at the expense of undiscovered needs of the community which thus have a double barrier to pass.

While professional education is ultimately concerned with *doing*, much other education is concerned with *being* – with understanding men in society, interpreting, evaluating, criticising, etc. Two disciplines neatly represent the interaction between the search for an over view, for long-term perspective, and for understanding, and also the urge to engage in specific social interaction: sociology and theology. The chapters in this book by Nancy Burton and Stephen Cotgrove, and by Anthony Dyson, not only deal with these subjects, but also discuss the value to students of a sandwich arrangement which encourages social service as part of the process of gaining understanding.

Arts subjects are traditionally justified as deepening understanding of the human condition through scholarship. Perhaps the deepening of the understanding of the select few can only be justified socially if this understanding is shared: in practice, in any case, very many arts graduates go into teaching. The chapters by Eric Hawkins and June Derrick, and by Geoffrey Summerfield therefore deal with their subjects largely from the point of view of the prospective teacher. It is a matter of great interest and concern that the education of prospective teachers leads to understanding not only of societies remote in time and space, but also of contemporary society. Social action may be the agency by which such understanding is acquired.

THE EDUCATIONAL AND SOCIAL ISSUES INVOLVED
IN EDUCATION THROUGH SOCIAL ACTION

The individual chapters of this book raise many specific educational and social issues relevant to particular forms of curriculum or of social action or of both. Some general issues are of such crucial importance in *any* form of education through social action that it is useful to extract them and comment on them. The seven areas of interest discussed below are ones of persistent, and often unresolved, difficulty.

(a) *What is community service?*
The two most obvious difficulties in discussing how Community Service and curriculum can be linked are to define first community and secondly service.

Bell and Newby (1971)[4] cite a paper by G. A. Hillery (1955), in which ninety-four separate definitions of community are given! For their own analysis, they perhaps wisely conclude that 'rather as intelligence is what intelligence tests measure, perhaps we can, for the time being at any rate, merely treat community as what Community Studies analyse' (page 32). But, for present purposes, it ery helpful to describe community as that sector of humanity served by trained minds. Clearly, commercial interests could well be supported by the curricular activities of students in higher education. There is, indeed, a lively debate still raging about the extent to which institutions of higher education should directly serve the needs of commerce as a method of indirectly serving the needs of mankind. When Cambridge men used to jibe that Oxford was 'the Latin quarter of Cowley', the remark was interpreted as a mere pleasantry. However, when a university is perceived as being *primarily* the extension of industrial interest, considerable bitterness may result. See for example *Warwick University Ltd*. edited by E. P. Thompson (1970).[5]

This is not to state dogmatically that Community Service cannot possibly take place through the agency of commerce. Indeed, the benevolent concern of commerce may be of prime importance in fostering the kind of imaginative educational experiments with which we are concerned. Voluntary activity may pioneer work which may later be seen as the legitimate interest of commerce. Similarly, voluntary activity has traditionally provided a goad to government. For example, the Department of the Environment has examined the ways in which voluntary organisations can achieve a multiplicity of worthwhile social purposes which currently fall into the interstices of statutory provision. The Department's report 'Fifty Million Volunteers' (1972)[6] illustrates the way in which the independent initiative of volunteers can highlight areas of social concern in which government may later become active.

Voluntary activity, perhaps financially aided by government, can create public opinion which, in turn, may generate statutory activity. A similar point has been urged by Adrian Moyes (1966, page 7)[7] who studied the activities of volunteers in developing countries and concluded: 'volunteers can be a useful form of technical assistance for development. They can fill genuine and important needs in developing countries; they can provide a valuable and relatively inexpensive addition to other technical assistance programmes. They have in addition, a helpful effect on domestic public opinion about developing countries and they are likely to promote international understanding. Many of them subsequently continue to work for developing countries.'

Volunteers do not necessarily give their services for nothing. The word volunteer simply indicates that their interest in the work they do is neither dictated by motives of commercial gain, nor by statute. Their work may, of course, produce commercial benefits and may provide a stimulus for government activity; that is not its motive. Not unnaturally, voluntary activity of one sort or another in this country concentrates on the needs of people who are educationally, physically, mentally, or otherwise deprived and those whose needs are not given the attention they deserve. It is this same sector of 'the community' with which the activities described in this book are concerned, and students may be seen as 'volunteers' in the sense suggested.

The areas of possible service by students in the course of their studies (or by anybody else for that matter) are legion. This is not the place for a catalogue of possible forms of service by students; rather, it is important to note two fundamental principles which should guide those who seek to serve.

Firstly, service must be *competent*. If Community Service is to have any real social relevance – be, in fact, more than a dilettante tinkering with irritants to the middle-class conscience – it will be affecting peoples' lives in some fundamental way. In his chapter, John Cartledge draws attention to some of the inherent difficulties of extra-curricula student community service and community action. For example, students are transient and service which demands sustained attention over a long period of time may simply not be possible. There is little point in looking to institutions of higher education for service if the service that can be given is unreliable or inefficient.

Secondly, service must be based on a principle of *reciprocity*. The dangers of 'do-goodery' are well known, and students go through agonies of conscience to avoid them. However, two other dangers are less often noticed. The first is that of 'academic voyeurism' in which well-heeled students from comfortable middle-class educational institutions go on forays into the concrete jungle and observe 'the natives', retreating to their centrally-heated halls of residence and writing elegant essays about deprivation. The cynical use of other people's miseries for academic data is only morally, not functionally, more reprehensible than dilettante dithering for genuine reasons of social concern. There is, then, a danger that institutions of higher education exploit those whom they seek to serve.

The second danger is the converse – that students may be exploited. Students may be used as anything from cheap labour to political pawns. Alan Barr (1972, page 126),[8] for example, has raised this point in connection with the 'bridge' year in which between leaving school and entering higher education, a student may spend a year working in and gaining experience of the 'real world'. Such experience is often gained in voluntary social service with Voluntary Service Overseas, Community Service Volunteers, and similar groups. Barr notes: 'at its highest level, the protagonists claim that the experience would provide for the development by the participant of an awareness to social need from which would begin an on-going concern. However, many critics believe that it would simply mean the exploitation of youthful enthusiasm in order to plug the gaps of an inadequate welfare state.'

The principle of reciprocity demands that each party to a social service arrangement has something worthwhile to gain from it. Clearly there are many social problems to which students in the course of their studies could apply the knowledge and skills which they are acquiring. This, one would hope, would be the benefit to those served. Contribution to education through the curriculum is the benefit one would hope students might enjoy.

(b) The curriculum of higher education and social purpose
What is the social purpose of universities? Any proposal to link direct social action to the curriculum forces attention to this question. The extreme positions are perhaps best stated in two phrases – on the one hand, that of Ernest Mandel (in Pateman, ed, 1972, page 19)[9] who says that: 'The university can be the cradle of a real revolution', and on the other, that of John Searle who, writing of *The Campus War* (1972)[10] speaks in favour of an aristocracy of the intellect. Mandel's view is of the university as a political institution ripe for revolution; Searle's is that of a specialised institution committed to detachment. By virtue of their cost, and their drain on public funds, universities are quite obviously political phenomena with political effects; and, of course, if any community service resulting from their activity causes genuine social change, that too would be of political significance. The important question is whether this new form of political involvement reinforces the university's value to society or derogates from it. It may be singularly unwise for universities to chase relevance which is subject to fashion. A 'Tom and Jerry' situation can soon develop in which a large and ungainly creature chases a small and nimble one, hideously mutilating itself in the process. If universities are to embark through education involving social action into a new type of humanitarian-

ism, as Alec Dickson advocates vigorously in the Foreword, it is wise to consider what may be sacrificed in the process.

It is possible to see the university as an oasis of objectivity in society. Its characteristic virtues are scholarship, precision, care. As with the real oasis, it is in everybody's interest not to foul the water. The social values implied in scholarship, in precise and careful attention to detail, accuracy and consistency, are just as real as the social values concerned with, for example, political power. There are, indeed, better organisations to effect social action – churches, political parties, pressure groups, public institutes, etc. Certainly, those who, by exposure to the curious practices of the universities, have acquired the taste for objectivity and detachment can go to these alternative organisations for direct social involvement. It is the specialised quality of the university's existence which leads John Searle to his concept of the aristocracy of the intellect. The university, he argues (page 203), 'is specialised in the way that hospitals, airlines, ski teams and brokerage houses are specialised; like them it has a limited set of objectives; and like them, it may, in the course of achieving its special objectives, enable its members to achieve incidentally all sorts of other subsidiary objectives – such as social improvement, happy sex life, political activity, etc. The goals are in the broad sense intellectual.' He goes on to argue that such a specialised institution dedicated to intellectual objectives is, by its very nature, not egalitarian. It does not place all its members on an equal footing, but rather makes a sharp distinction between the masters and the apprentices, between the professionals and the aspirants. 'To mark these two features of the university, its intellectual objectives, and its inherent class structure, I prefer to characterise it as an aristocracy of the intellect.'

It is this same modesty of social objective that concerns Robert Nisbet in *The Degradation of the Academic Dogma* (1971).[11] He writes (page 228): 'It is no more possible for the university to serve all individual needs and tastes than it is possible for it to serve all social, economic and political needs in society.' Both Searle and Nisbet attribute the widespread disruption of American university life in the 1960s to neglect of what they see as the university's primary function.

Yet, however much one may value the specialised nature of the university's work, it is still necessary for the individual who works in the university, as student or teacher, to have some conception of the social relevance of his activity, to have a motive for being there at all; and this may best be achieved through some direct involvement with community problems. Only in this way can the substance of the university's intellectual activity be socially informed. In like manner, it is important that the community which pays for the activities of the university gets whatever benefit it can from the precise and careful processes of scholarship.

There is a major dilemma in education through social action. The university approach to knowledge is valued for its attempt at objectivity and dispassionate evaluation of all facets of a problem; yet the application of this approach to specific social problems through direct social action may destroy the very conditions for which the approach is valued. Both the long- and the short-term benefits which universities can bring to society may be lost if their unique commitment to detachment becomes blurred. Boundary maintenance and intellectual territoriality may have something to commend them: a college is not a church. As Sir Walter Moberly put it some years ago (1949, page 39)[12] 'A university is a "thought organisation" not a "will organisation" and its aim is understanding rather than action. It is a society for the pursuit of knowledge and not for the promotion of this cause or the prevention of that abuse.'

If universities are to retain their credibility as organisations with a highly defined, and socially valuable, intellectual purpose, it is vital that both educational and social objectives be clearly *stated* if programmes of education through social action are being contemplated.

(c) *The enigma of professional education*

Since the foundation of universities in medieval Europe, professional education has gone on within their walls. Paradoxically, the demands of professions for consensus in knowledge represent the most acute challenge to the university's commitment to detachment, scholarship, and dispassionate criticism. It is precisely at this point that education through social action, as a form of professional education, challenges the concept of consensus. In a curious way, community involvement which, it has just been argued, can represent a threat to the fundamental academic dogma at the same time may be the agency whereby professional education is redirected and made more self critical.

Judith Allen and John A. D. Palmer in their chapter 'Community Service and Community Planning – Whose Ideals?' raise this issue directly. But, as Edgar H. Schein has argued in *Professional Educa-*

tion: Some New Directions (1972)[13] the issue is one which pervades the whole of professional education. Where professional associations define criteria of admission, educational standards, licensing or other formal entry examinations, career lines within a profession and areas of jurisdiction for the profession, there is a tendency for a professional mystique to develop whereby areas of choice are not necessarily made explicit to a client and he is constrained to operate only through the offices of a professional. The education of intending professionals through social action should make them more sensitive to the beliefs, motivations and wishes of those they will later serve. This increased social awareness should help the young professional to be more explicit about whose interests any action will serve. Detachment, in the sense of dispassionate evaluation of a multiplicity of alternatives, is thus fostered by social action which, if ineptly handled, can engender intellectual confusion.

How is suitable social involvement to be achieved?

(d) The value of the sandwich principle
Some form of sandwich arrangement (ranging from days in a week to months in a year) may be a logistic necessity if social action is to be combined with more traditional modes of education. Indeed, the sandwich principle of education has a long and distinguished history in subjects like engineering. Its value is emphasised in the chapters of this book by Nancy Burton and Stephen Cotgrove, and by Anthony Dyson. In sociology, Burton and Cotgrove argue that the exposure to practical social problems deepens students' understanding of the social theories which they encounter in their sociology. Likewise, the interaction of social service and theological studies provides perspective in theology. In any discipline, it should be obvious that theory is largely meaningless without experience, as experience is in the deepest sense unintelligible without theory. Even if contemplation, rather than doing, is seen as the principal virtue of higher education (for example, in the humanities) there is questionable wisdom in extracting a student from the community for three years at a stretch. It is for this reason that Geoffrey Summerfield argues forcefully against the isolation of the intending teacher of English from the community which he is later going to serve.

It has sometimes been argued that the university provides a retreat from the world in which the student can contemplate and evaluate his social experience. Perhaps, nowadays, it could be argued that a student needs to retreat from the university to digest the ideas he has encountered there. Indeed, Peter Marris writing of *The Experience of Higher Education* (1964)[14] has suggested that detachment from his community in a university institution can be a profoundly alienating experience for a student: 'Unless a student can overcome this sense of alienation, his university experience will not enable him to establish his identity within society at large. Higher education seems to most students to divorce them intellectually from their background and project them towards a status in society uncomfortably enviable; they need time to untangle their conflicting loyalties, and take their stand' (page 141).

The sandwich principle of education, then, it can be argued, is not only educationally valuable in deepening a student's understanding of his subject; it can also provide him with the opportunity to re-identify himself with the community from which he has come by practical service to it, and thereby strengthen his apprehension of the social as well as intellectual value of his university experience.

(e) Educating the educators
Eric Midwinter has shown, in his chapter on 'Student Help for the Educationally Disadvantaged', how effective the sandwich principle can be. Service in schools is a form of limited social involvement in which students are kept on a very short lead, and which by this very fact seems to have been profoundly effective. It is an attractive idea to see the *educational* system, through which every student has, by definition, progressed as being the first area in which community service may be contemplated. Like Eric Midwinter, Eric Hawkins and June Derrick in the chapter 'Summer projects for Children with Language Difficulties' argue that this concept of the helping hand is an extremely promising one. Not only is an immediate and desperately needed form of social service rendered in community institutions which students understand, but also the learning of the students is by that very fact reinforced. It is well known that the best way to learn a subject is to teach it. There is, however, an even more intriguing possibility in the marriage of community service and the curriculum in higher education. That is that those whom students seek to serve through their curricular activities become *ipso facto* educators. If the principle of reciprocity is to be respected in any form of community service linked with the curriculum in higher education, it must be seen that those who are given service by students are contributing to the education of

the students. Anyone who receives service is, therefore, an educator. As I see it, this goes some way to meeting the objective which Ivan Illich states rather dramatically and provocatively in *Deschooling Society* (1971).[15] Illich suggests the rather drastic measure of removing schools as special institutions from society because everyone suffers in a situation where schools are regarded as the only places in which learning can take place. The school, Illich argues, is just the age-specific, teacher-related process requiring full-time attendance at an obligatory curriculum. Schools deprive the community of the privilege and duty to share wisdom with the young, and deprive the young of the richness of exposure which community involvement could provide. If community service can indeed become involved in the curriculum of higher education, one might hope to see an educational function being regarded as part of the normal activity of every servicing organisation. Hospitals, old people's homes, prisons, etc. might be expected to devote part of their resources to ensuring that education was provided in some systematic and sensitive way to those who, as part of their curriculum, offered service within those institutions.

(f) The assessment of community-related curricula
A thorny issue, which appears in several chapters which follow, is that of the assessment for degree marks of community-related curricula. The tension is between validity and reliability. Universities have, at present, the task of providing credentials (in the form of degrees, certificates, etc.) to students, which form currency for a wide variety of occupations. The concept of university as ticket machine is an exaggeration too near the truth to be funny.

Assessment has three functions: firstly to let the student know whether he is achieving the objectives which he has set himself; secondly to let the teacher know whether his intervention in the learning process has been effective; and thirdly to let the teacher know if the student has met the teacher's learning objective. It is on this last criterion that the grading of students' performances is carried out. But in activities where the outcome is unknown in detail to the supervisor as to the student, this sort of assessment cannot be done with any reliability. John Brown and I, in our chapter on engineering education, point to the dilemma, that the requirement for a reliable form of assessment (for a degree class) may militate against an educationally viable and valid activity. Community service curricula force to attention the question: Are we to assume that the only valid forms of university activity are those which can be assessed reliably?

Many suggestions are currently being offered in this difficult dilemma. For example, C. C. Butler, writing in *What Kinds of Graduates Do we Need?*, edited by F. R. Jevons and H. D. Turner (1972, page 90–1)[16] examines the possible use of profiles to replace degree classes.

The assignment of a degree class 1, 2, 3 or 'pass' as the sole indication of achievement in three years of highly complex study, involving a wide range of taxing intellectual activities, is at best crude and at worst largely meaningless. If the pressure on universities to produce credentials in the form of degree classes were to be removed, and some form of profile to take the place of the degree, community-related curricula would be easier to adopt. In the meantime, suffice it to note that the attempt to link community service with the curriculum in higher education forces attention to the many difficulties of assessment.

(g) The ethos of the university
Several of the chapters which follow point to the crucial importance of faculty supervision of community-related curricula. For example, Nancy Burton and Stephen Cotgrove point to the need for a professional administrator of student placements in the sandwich course of sociology. Such a person must necessarily understand the teaching process and objectives of the university while at the same time being involved in a mass of detailed administration. In R. K. Merton's language, such an administrator will almost by definition be a local rather than a cosmopolitan. That is to say, the key administrator must be deeply committed to the service rendered by the teaching institution and by the fertilisation of the teaching activity through the experience of direct social action. In practically any form of activity which one can think of, such responsibility is so severe that extensive scholarship or research becomes difficult. There is a widespread ethos in universities in which 'international visibility' has high prestige, while service to the teaching function of the institution has low prestige. The American phrase 'publish or perish' describes this.

If the linking of community service and the curriculum in higher education is to be effective, either the ethos prevailing in universities will have to be ignored, or a new academic value will have to be pioneered – that of research not as the finding of new knowledge but as the achievement of understanding through the spreading and using of existing knowledge in hitherto untouched social situations. Once again, the tensions involved in community-related curricula may provide a new dynamic for universities.

These general academic issues are perhaps the ones which should most exercise universities if, as is to be hoped, the interest in developing community service and social action in the context of the curriculum grows. Whatever universities do, they will be regarded as politically compromised by one sector or the other. Either they will be lashed by the left for grovelling obsequiously in the market-place or they will be castigated by the right for dreaming dreadful dreams of revolution in their ivory towers. Perhaps, therefore, it is the central and highly specialised nature of their intellectual endeavour which should be most vividly borne in mind when new fields of activity are contemplated.

No other institutions in society are committed to detachment and dispassionate intellectual activity as universities are. And, as Robert Nisbet has argued, it is the ideal which is important – it is an ideal which informs the work of polytechnics, colleges of education, theological colleges and other educational institutions. Whatever may be the political or social motivation behind them, their central task is that of criticism, of pointing up areas of choice, of handling information, of transmitting skills. These things they do well; they are less good at generating political action or religious fervour.

Yet, however desirable it may be to foster one element of personality, the intellect, intensively in higher education, it is imperative not to neglect the others. Perhaps what one is seeking educationally is best summed up in the words of Nevitt Sandford writing in *Higher Education: Demand and Response*, edited by W. R. Niblett (1969, page 10)[17]: '. . . educators might say competence is to be developed in schools, compassion in other institutions. But personality functions as a whole; virtues are interrelated; and actions to promote one will have consequences for others. From the point of view of personality theory what is most to be desired is a state that favours high development in many virtues and a chance for superlative development in some, and that does not lead to serious neglect of any; this state is one of complexity and wholeness in the person.' This wholeness in the person is clearly the benefit which a student may hope to gain from community service. The crucial task in planning education through social action is to ensure that balance is achieved, that neither is intellectual incisiveness muddied by emotion nor is 'the native hue of resolution sicklied o'er by the pale caste of thought'.

If viable ways of linking community service and the curriculum in higher education can be found, a huge reservoir of talent is at the disposal of those seeking various social objectives. The chapters which follow tentatively explore a few areas in a vast and a complex field.

One last comment may be appropriate. In the business of staying alive, it is easy to neglect the reasons for doing so. Education is not only a means to an end; it is an end in itself. All forms of humane cultural manipulation are ultimately motivated by a desire to share a wholeness and richness of experience which is the very substance of education. If the values of education are destroyed in the process, the world will not have been well lost. Again the words of Nevitt Sandford (page 11): 'Just as in the larger world culture and (sometimes) technology can serve man so in a university research, scholarship, professional training and direct service to society should be carried out in such a way as to serve educational purposes. If these activities contribute nothing to education they might as well be done elsewhere; if they interfere with education they were better done elsewhere.'

THE ARRANGEMENT OF THE CHAPTERS

John Cartledge's chapter on 'Student, College and Community' examines the concepts and practices of student community service and community action, emphasising the distinction between the approaches, and reviewing what has been attempted and what has been achieved in extra-curricular activities. He analyses some of the frustrations experienced by students and some of the inadequacies of their initiatives which stem from the division of loyalties involved in purely spare-time work. Only when social action arises directly from education will these difficulties be resolved.

Eric Midwinter offers a consumer's-eye-view of the participation by education students as part of their curriculum in a project with specific social objectives. He makes the crucial point that not only does social action arise from the students' education, but also that the education of students benefits from this work. Everyone should benefit from a scheme of education through social action, and his chapter illustrates vividly how students of education learn about priority education by helping with it.

Geoffrey Summerfield, too, deals with the intending teacher. Writing of 'The Student of Literature and the Needs of Children', he stresses the value of some sort of community involvement for all intending teachers. The teacher of English in particular must learn to understand the fabric, rhythms, tensions, and idioms of the daily lives of his pupils, so that he will not treat pupils speaking a non-standard dialect as in some way 'deprived'. The way of empathy, he argues, rests on the teacher's responsiveness to his pupils, to who they are and to where they are. Such empathy is acquired not from scholarly criticism of set texts but from sensitive sharing of primary experience.

Michael Zander discusses the potential value of 'clinical' studies in British legal education and evaluates the educational and social value of student participation in legal advice services. His chapter on 'Law Students and Community Action' gives many examples of American practice which would be a useful model for Britain. He stresses the intellectual challenge, to students, of real-life situations where problems are not divided into the neat categories of law teachers. Voluntary, unpaid work may be an important first step to clinical studies, but the real value of clinical studies is that they combine a much-needed form of community service with a highly effective mode of law education.

Judith Allen and John Palmer, in their chapter 'Community Service and Community Planning', raise important questions about the nature of 'public service' as interpreted in town planning. Examining the fundamentally political nature of the planning process, they discuss the re-alignment of attitudes in teaching, such as a non-authoritarian approach, which is appropriate in a context where political power in the community has been redistributed. In community planning, they argue, the primary reference group for the planner is the community group with whom he is working – not the planning profession or government. The model of teaching – involving the transfer of expertise from the professional to the non-professional – becomes, they argue, the model for the planning process. In the light of their re-interpretation of the planner's role, they then examine the conditions which are the necessary basis for community fieldwork.

John Brown and I discuss 'Community-related Project Work in Engineering'. The specifications for any system or device designed by an engineer are socially derived; indeed, the most difficult task for the engineer is to formulate a specification which does full justice to the economic and social constraints on the system. We show how community-related project work can not only result in systems or devices of some immediate practical value, but can also deepen a student's understanding of his technical skills.

In education, law, town planning and engineering the result of intellectual endeavour is a service to a client. It is not difficult to show how education through social action can render valuable practical service as well as widen the student's knowledge of the range of potential clients and the variety of their needs. The activities described in Chapters 2 to 6 can deepen a student's sensitivity to the human complexities of society before a professional hardening of the arteries sets in under the influence of his professional association. But what of disciplines which offer a general education, not immediately related to the operational requirements of a specific occupation? How can education through social action meet non-vocational objectives?

Anthony Dyson's discussion of 'Fieldwork in Theological Education' is of central importance in this context, and thus in the book as a whole. Theology is both a disciplined form of consciousness of general educational interest and value and also part of the intellectual background of a priest. By discussing the role of the priest as a professional, Anthony Dyson's chapter provides a bridge between vocational and non-vocational education and raises directly the problem of the supposed conflict between 'academic' and 'practical' aspects of training. Where practical activities are possible and desirable additions to theorising, there is a danger of escape from fundamental questions into busyness. Anthony Dyson shows how a student priest must explore how a critical appreciation of the gospel (theological studies) relates to a critical appreciation of man in his contemporary environment (social studies), and how each critically relates to, and is related by, an appreciation of ministerial and churchly activity (pastoral studies). The methodological problems of achieving this blend of the academic and the practical are of interest and importance in many disciplines. Anthony Dyson describes the interplay of participant observation of social situations and intensive seminars which might be taken as a model for subjects other than theology. The case for *concurrent* practical work and reflection he regards as proved.

These tactics may be the best for use in a strategy of education through social action if effective *action* is to be achieved; they may also constitute the most effective *heuristic* procedure if *reflection* is the principal aim.

Substantially the same point is made by *Nancy Burton and Stephen Cotgrove* in their description of 'A Sandwich Course in Sociology'. Sociology is both a theoretical study of conceptual systems and an attempt to develop scientific methods of measurement and analysis to problems of social engineering. Theory and practice are symbiotic; direct experience of small-scale social systems which a student can achieve through community service or community action helps him to see the relevance of theory, just as the theory helps him to interpret and understand the social situations with which he has to cope. The sandwich arrangement which they discuss may be the only practical way of combining study and service if competent and whole-hearted service is to be combined with deep thought.

The 'Summer Projects for Children with Language Difficulties' described by *Eric Hawkins and June Derrick* are not, at the time of writing, part of the curriculum of the students who take part in them. But the authors argue that the cultural and linguistic insights achieved by the students as they help immigrant children to acquire greater social knowledge and linguistic confidence are of obvious relevance to their studies – particularly if those studies are in languages or the social sciences.

Finally, *David Brockington* discusses some examples of 'Community Action in Liberal Studies'. In many technical colleges, liberal studies are taught as a 'civilising' influence. Typically, liberal studies occupy 10 to 15 per cent of a student's time and the teacher is supposed, in that time, to bring about an enrichment of his students' lives of the sort that full-time attendance at an arts degree course should achieve. David Brockington describes how the building of an adventure playground not only met certain urgent social objectives, but was effective as a teaching *method* within his terms of reference as a liberal studies teacher.

It would be inappropriate and misleading to attempt a concise summary of the collective message of the chapters of this book. Not only do widely different educational objectives appear in the disciplines represented, but widely different social and political philosophies inform the various types of community service and community action discussed. Whether universities are seen as service stations or sanctuaries, whether their contribution to social

c

living is believed to be direct or indirect, intelligently conceived schemes can combine genuine education with urgently needed social action.

REFERENCES

1 J. S. R. Goodlad, *Science for Non-Scientists*, Oxford University Press, 1973.
2 Schools Council, *Community Service and the Curriculum*, Working Paper No. 17, HMSO, London, 1968.
3 G. Brosan, *et al.*, *Patterns and Policies in Higher Education*, Penguin, Harmondsworth, 1971.
4 C. Bell and H. Newby, *Community Studies*, George Allen & Unwin, London, 1971.
5 E. P. Thompson (ed), *Warwick University Ltd*, Penguin, Harmondsworth, 1970.
6 Department of the Environment, *Fifty Million Volunteers*, HMSO, London, 1972.
7 Adrian Moyes, *Volunteers in Development*, Overseas Development Institute, London, 1966.
8 Alan Barr, *Student Community Action*, National Council of Social Service, Bedford Square Press, London, 1972.
9 T. Pateman (ed), *Counter Course: A Handbook for Course Criticism*, Penguin, Harmondsworth, 1972.
10 John Searle, *The Campus War*, Penguin, Harmondsworth, 1972.
11 Robert Nisbet, *The Degradation of the Academic Dogma*, Heinemann Educational Books, London, 1971.
12 Sir Walter Moberly, *The Crisis in the University*, SCM Press, London, 1949.
13 E. H. Schein, *Professional Education: Some New Directions*, The Carnegie Commission on Higher Education, McGraw Hill, London, 1972.
14 Peter Marris, *The Experience of Higher Education*, Routledge & Kegan Paul, London, 1964.
15 Ivan D. Illich, *Deschooling Society*, Calder & Boyars, London, 1971.
16 F. R. Jevons and H. D. Turner (eds), *What Kinds of Graduates Do We Need?*, Oxford University Press, 1972.
17 W. R. Niblett (ed), *Higher Education: Demand and Response*, Tavistock, London, 1969.

Chapter One

Student, College and Community

BY JOHN CARTLEDGE

John Cartledge teaches at Edgware School. Since graduating in Geography at Cambridge University, he has taken a Certificate of Education and been Secretary to the Cambridge University Graduate Society, spent a year as Director of the London Organisation for Student Community Action and served on the permanent staff of Community Service Volunteers. He is a member of the new Hertfordshire County Council.

'The only way to know conditions is to make social investigations, to investigate the social conditions of each class in real life. Such investigation is especially necessary for those who know theory but do not know the actual conditions, for otherwise they will not be able to link theory with practice. Reading is learning, but applying is also learning and the more important kind of learning at that. When in addition to reading some Marxist books our intellectuals have gained some understanding through close contact with the masses of peasants and workers and through their own practical work, we will all be speaking the same language.'[1]

'The universities are increasingly aware that they cannot survive in a society which does not resolve its festering injustices. An education is not complete unless it includes an awareness of contemporary social problems. To be a positive force for positive change – to help break the barriers – student volunteers must approach their tasks with open eyes and open minds. Every institution or organisation in society is involved in supporting or altering the status quo, and students must be aware of which ones share their own aims and motives most fully. They must also have a clear understanding of what they hope will be achieved in the realm of social change.'[2]

A belief in the possibility and desirability of close practical links between the higher education system and movements for social change is a worldwide phenomenon, transcending differences of political ideology and social structure. The first quotation above is taken from the Thoughts of Chairman Mao-Tse Tung, the second from a manual published by the US Government Printing Office, but the coincidence of view is remarkable. More remarkable still, in view of the global extent of this connection, is the apparent ease with which British universities and colleges have stood aside from this trend, and the insignificance of the organised student movement as a social force outside the narrow limits of its immediate institutional environment. British academics have never displayed any active concern for the needs of 'the community', or their relationship with it – except insofar as the term is used in a general way to denote society at large. The idyllic vision of a 'community of scholars' has inescapable overtones of introversion and introspection, a withdrawal from the hurly-burly of real-life conflicts and pressures into the sheltered, quasi-monastic calm of the academic ivory tower. The history of universities' dealings with the state has been one of a long and largely successful struggle to preserve freedom of thought and study from 'improper' pressure and direction from elsewhere, and, despite their near total reliance upon public funds for all purposes, the universities still continue strenuously to resist any but the most general directions from official quarters regarding their purposes and work.

And if central government has been kept at arm's length, local government has been kept almost wholly out of sight. An elderly alderman or two can generally be found amongst the ranks of the (purely ceremonial) court of governors with perhaps an industrialist and a (usually retired) trade unionist thrown in for good measure. But even this token connection is of comparatively recent origin. It is interesting to note that until now the symbolic connection has been reversed in the two oldest English universities, with oligarchic committees of college bursars appointing eight of their number to serve on the respective city councils. Certainly, any suggestion that the local community might have some prior claim upon the universities' time and resources would be vigorously denied. The recent suggestion of both Labour and Conservative Education Ministers that English universities might move closer to the Scottish (or French) pattern of regionalised intake and a substantial proportion of home-based students was greeted with a unanimous outburst of vice-chancellorial hostility. And the new generation of technological universities differs little. The former CATs were distinguished by the speed with which – upon receipt of their royal charters and consequent elevation to true university status – they jettisoned their sub-degree level and vocational courses, and hence their curricular orientation to the needs of their host communities. And notwithstanding the claims of their dwindling army of protagonists and their different administrative structures, precisely the same traits are now being exhibited by the great majority of polytechnics. Only at Bath and Loughborough universities have there been signs of a possible reversal in this trend, with the setting up of limited liability trading companies to advertise the availability of university research facilities to local industry. But since the object of these enterprises is simply to make available their intellectual plus physical resources to the highest commercial bidder, far from their being signs of incipient 'community relatedness' in the sense advocated by radical critics of academic monasticism, they are merely the most conspicuous symbols of some universities' readiness to prostitute themselves to the needs and wishes of corporate capitalism – an intellectual servitude which was dramatically exemplified by the revelation of the relationship between the administrations of Warwick University and Chrysler (United Kingdom) in 1970.[3] In short, the present situation is one in which, though institutions of higher education dot the landscape on all sides, such connection as they may have with the local community which surrounds them is purely symbolic and peripheral. In both their academic and social policies (social here implying such matters as student housing arrangements, recreational provision, wage policies for non-academic employees and the like) they are, at best, indifferent to local needs and views and, at worst, quite as insensitive and hostile as major industrial enterprises, property companies or similarly powerful and non-accountable social institutions.

It is interesting, in passing, to compare this situation with that in the United States, since, notwithstanding Britain's recent conspicuously unenthusiastic lurch into (Western) Europe, it seems likely that the US will continue for some time to be our largest single source of intellectual stimulus and area of academic intercourse (if only by default because the academic structures of most EEC countries are yet more elitist and socially unaccountable than our own). It is, of course, difficult to generalise about the nature and character of higher education in a system as gigantic and variegated as the American, and it undoubtedly includes a number of institutions where overt evidence of concern with questions of social responsibility is as lacking as in Britain. But it is true to say that at the administrative level the 'Vice-President for Community Affairs' – or some comparable post – has in the last decade become a common feature of many campuses, and in a number of cases the process has been carried much further. At Wayne State University in downtown Detroit, for example, the entire curriculum has been reoriented towards the needs of the ghetto community in which it is located. The City University of New York, with its adoption of a complete open-admissions policy, has now entered the field of mass community education on a grand scale, while Harvard's much publicised controversy over the impact of its expansion plans on the low-income residents of surrounding neighbourhoods has been paralleled by comparable conflicts in many other institutions. In the case of Columbia, the competing claims of the university for building land and of Harlem residents for recreational open space led to open confrontation and the temporary paralysis of the institution.

Welcome though these developments are in their own right, it is arguable whether they would have occurred had they not been preceded by the tide of student revolt which swept across the campuses in the late 1960s. The revolts themselves were short-lived, and their single most important cause – mass conscription for the US forces in Vietnam – has been removed, but the mark they have left is indelible, and the heightened social awareness of both faculty and students is a part of their enduring legacy. Many US colleges, at any rate those operated under public auspices, have always had an element of community orientation in their character, deriving from the limited geographical area from which a majority of their students are drawn and the local origin of their administration and finance. But this relationship has been dramatically reinforced by the welter of practical student community action programmes which have flourished in the aftermath of the strikes, sit-ins and protests of recent years. According to the National Student Volunteer Program (NSVP) headquarters in Washington, a recent Gallup poll showed that approximately 400,000 students on 1,700 campuses are now regularly involved in some form of voluntary social action.[4] The range recorded is enormous – from free breakfasts for slum kids to law-for-laymen seminars, from drug hotlines to 'adopt-a-grandparent' schemes, from job scouts for ex-prisoners to 'project price watch', from food co-operatives to eco-action squads – and so too is the extent to which they are concerned with promoting measurable social change, as opposed to mere short-term relief. But the promotion of change is not regarded as a sinister political aberration (as the extract from an NSVP manifesto at the head of this chapter revealed) and the favour with which such activities are regarded by academic authorities can be measured in their response to NSVP's most recent experiment, the University Year for Action. This is a scheme whereby students are permitted to take a year off from their normal courses to work as full-time volunteers in social action projects, yet still receive full academic credit. In its pilot stage, UYA had already enrolled 1,000 students from twenty-four colleges, in all parts of the country, and the enthusiastic response of its first batch of recruits seemed certain to guarantee it an expanded role in the future.[5]

Clearly, the sheer size of the United States, and the flexibility of its colleges' academic crediting arrangements, make an operation of this style and scope far easier to mount than in Britain. But practical considerations of this kind are only a partial explanation of British universities' total failure – so far – to show any but the most token interest in student community action ventures. Equally important, it must be admitted, are their tradition-bound limits to the proper scope of academic activity, their largely theoretical curricula, and their general unconcern for students' extra-mural and extra-curricular activities. The call for student union autonomy – in itself desirable – has been misinterpreted as an argument for a total separation between in-class and out-of-class activities, with the inevitable result that the claims of student community activists for a share of universities' formal teaching time and curricular resources have been largely ignored. A survey of heads of departments conducted at the Queen's University, Belfast, in 1972 revealed starkly the degree to which they were indifferent (if not actually hostile) to the proposition that, in as dramatic a situation of social unrest as that which prevails in Northern Ireland, the University might be neglecting its responsibilities to the wider community by failing to seek ways in which it could contribute directly to the resolution of some of the underlying social conflicts.[6] It is clear from their replies that conventionally assessed criteria of 'academic merit' were the chief preoccupation of this particular cross-section of academics and there is no reason to believe that their counterparts elsewhere are very different. Only such vocationally-oriented disciplines as law, medicine and architecture laid claim to any significant degree of community-relatedness in their curricula – and none of these did so in the specific context of the immediate needs of the local community.

It would be quite wrong to imply from all this, however, that social concern of any kind is wholly alien to the British academic tradition. Rather, it has been relegated to a well-established but essentially peripheral backwater, from which it is extremely difficult to restore it to the mainstream of university life and thought. The university-sponsored 'settlements' (located, as a rule, far from the institutions which spawned them) still survive as independent social work agencies in East London, Liverpool, Birmingham and elsewhere and most still receive a measure of financial support from their parent bodies, though the breed of earnest undergraduates of half a century ago, who helped to run their scout troops and their old folks' treats, has, for the most part, disappeared. The time-honoured tradition of the rag is now also in decline – partly because of public hostility to students in general, but partly too because of diminished student interest in fund raising activities of a kind in which the efforts of the participants are only very distantly and ephemerally related to the chosen causes. Charitable fund raising, however enjoyable the techniques employed may be in themselves, appears very much a second best to students who seek a more direct and personal engagement in tackling social needs of every kind. And in many places open conflicts have arisen where students have sought to change the list of beneficiaries, since the local authorities which licence street collections have from time to time vetoed the omission of a well known national charity such as the Haig Fund in favour of causes closer to the students' own experience or interests. In such situations, the usual consequence has been the abandonment of the rag and the diversion of the student energies into work on behalf of the group (for example, an advice centre for young people with drug problems, or gypsy support group, to take two recent examples) to which exception has been taken by the licensing authority. Though firm evidence is hard to come by, it seems likely that a comparable decline in support has affected the work-camps which once attracted large numbers of young people from different countries to live and work together on some common task (generally of a constructional character) during their vacations. The reasons for this are less easy to explain, but one might hazard a guess that as international travel has ceased to be a privilege of an affluent elite and hitchhiking across continents becomes almost commonplace, it is no longer necessary for young people to seek the organised and structured system of the work-camp in order to meet their peers from other countries and to see the world.

But as these patterns of activity have declined, so new manifestations of students' social concern have arisen to take their place. 'Student community action' is a fairly recent addition to the jargon of educational debate, but in the late 1960s and early 1970s its protagonists have established themselves as a significant element within the British student movement. To some extent, it is an outgrowth of the older traditions of social service already described, but whereas they were almost invariably religious rather than political in inspiration, the present generation of student community activists have tended to express their aims in unreservedly political terms, and to affect a style of activity and argument far more closely related to that of the contemporary generation of radical student leaders. Indeed, the growth of SCA can be shown to be directly in the mainstream of student militancy, insofar as once the immediate grievances over the more trivial restrictions on students' life styles had been resolved, and a measure of participation in university and college government secured (albeit generally only in the marginal areas of decision making), it was not unnatural that students' attention should turn to the relationship between their institutions and the wider society of which they are a part. Those students who are alienated from a society devoted very largely to the pursuit of purely materialist aims, organised on a competitive and individualistic basis, yet increasingly indifferent to fundamental problems of civil liberties and intolerant of non-conforming and culturally independent minorities – these students have naturally been foremost amongst the critics of institutions which, while purporting to protect the fundamental values of freedom in thought, research, speech and writing, appear, in practice, to have become little more than the agencies of the corporate capitalist state, processing a carefully selected elite to occupy positions of power and profit in society tomorrow. Assertions of this kind, declaimed before student audiences to thunderous applause, are characterised as a rule by remarkable woolliness of thought – and it is fair to question how far their advocates can, in practice, claim to speak for the generality of students, since they themselves are apt to make frequent reference to the need to raise the 'level of consciousness' of their peers. But it cannot be gainsaid that a serious debate about the total social role of the higher education system is taking place today within the leadership of the organised student movement, quite distinct from its day-to-day concern with grants, accommodation, social facilities, admissions procedures and the like – and that central to this debate is a widespread conviction that, by some means, student radicals must make common cause with other forces of dissent and movements for change within society.

The ephemerality of the student experience and the generally limited day-to-day contact of students with groups outside the formal system of higher education are major obstacles to the forging of effective and enduring links – coupled with a not unnatural scepticism, on the part of many 'grass root' community groups, towards the students' real intentions. It is not difficult for intelligent, articulate, socially-conscious students to perceive in the sudden flourishing of tenants' associations, claimants unions, free schools, pre-school playgroups, neighbourhood councils, community newspapers and the like, a striking upswell of political activity within the community wholly outside the conventional and now discredited partisan framework – and to seek to identify with it. But it is sometimes more difficult for the members of such groups to see in students (who may appear, at least superficially, to be in some respects a privileged stratum within society) their natural allies, not least because of students' often limited acquaintance with and understanding of the communities within and alongside which they seek to work. And such reservations about the intentions or, indeed, the worth of students as allies in such campaigns tend to be reinforced by the frequent failure of students to fulfil the commitments they have entered into. There are innumerable examples of instances where students (with the best of intentions) have accepted leadership roles in local groups, only to disappear on vacation for five months or more each year, leaving the group in a situation worse than that which would have obtained had they not intervened in the first place. In his account of the Liverpool Educational Priority Area Project, for example, Eric Midwinter has much to say in favour of the student teachers who – in this case, unusually, under the guidance and with the support of their colleges – took part in the programme of experimental curricular innovations which the Project was set up to promote. But he makes no attempt to conceal his frustration and annoyance at the self-selected student group which volunteered to undertake the running of a 'community festival' only to disappear on vacation at a critical stage and all but sabotage the entire venture.[7]

Another problem arises where the students conceptualise the ultimate objectives of the work in which they are engaged in terms very different from those of the non-student groups in the community with which they are working. Most student community activists, it is fair to say, are probably committed to a belief in the need for fairly fundamental changes in the total pattern of society, including a far greater measure of control by ordinary citizens over the decisions which critically affect their lives. As a worker, man (if not yet woman) is comparatively well organised via the agency of his trade union and through this his vital interests are protected. But man as tenant, man as consumer and man as recipient of social welfare services, tends, as a rule, to be much less well protected against the pressures of powerful and hostile social forces, and has little direct say in the administration of the services which so centrally affect his well-being. It is in this sphere that the student community activists are seeking to change the structures and institutions where the community groups themselves may be seeking nothing more than to improve their efficiency and perhaps to make their methods of operation more humane. A good example of this is afforded by the experience of the family squatting movement, which set out to persuade local authorities in areas of acute housing stress to make vacant property awaiting demolition available to otherwise homeless families. In the initial stages, when confrontations with police or bailiffs were frequent and there was little evidence of widespread public interest in or sympathy for the squatters' plight, a substantial measure of student support was attracted to their cause. But once most of the local authorities concerned had reversed their policies and entered into agreements making suitable properties available to squatters on a short term basis (thus conveniently reducing the level of demand on the councils' own homeless family accommodation) the glamour attached to the squatters' cause was dissipated and, for the most part, the students drifted off into other campaigns. For many, perhaps, the purely existential excitement of confrontation gave satisfaction in itself and the nature of the cause at stake was of only secondary significance. But for others, there was undoubtedly a deeper significance attached to this particular pattern of community action, in that it might possibly have signified the first stirrings in a far more widespread protest over the entire archaic and unjust system of property ownership and housing provision which obtains. In the event, the squatters campaign was no more successful than the more recent efforts to obstruct the enforcement of the Housing Finance Act, which is designed to convert council housing into a source of profit for the local and central government authorities, and thus to subsidise ratepayers at the expense of council tenants. The fundamental conservatism of British society is far too strongly entrenched to be shaken by minor tribulations of this kind and the idealistic student radical retires defeated to face a simple choice – whether to resign himself to inaction and despair, or whether to turn instead to community service as the best available alternative.

The distinction here is an important one. Community action denotes efforts by disadvantaged or deprived groups within society to gain greater control over, or at least materially to influence, decisions which affect their lives – whereas community service is merely some form of activity which improves the immediate material lot of such groups without affecting the basic patterns of power relationships in society.[8] But community action is difficult to initiate and sustain except in quite exceptional circumstances – such as the threat to the property values of Vale of Aylesbury commuters represented by the projected construction at Cublington of London's third airport, to take a highly successful if sociologically untypical case – whereas community service can be performed in almost any place at any time, and does at least attract a measure of social approbation. Radical students will often denounce it as mere 'wall-papering', that is, the temporary obscuring of defects in social fabric which requires total reconstruction, but they tend in practice to find themselves in roles precisely of this kind. Thus it is noticeable how a degree of schizophrenia has run through much of the discussion and debate on student community action so far – the will for societal change and political action is undoubtedly there and frequently reasserted – yet the action itself is generally of a service-oriented character. Only in a limited number of places have students yet shown themselves to be capable of sustaining on-going programmes of a more overtly political kind, not least because student union funds (on which the majority of projects are wholly or largely dependent for their income) are regarded by the courts as having the same charitable status as that of the parent university or college under whose constitution the union is established, and for this reason the unions are constrained from spending money on purposes not directly beneficial to their own members.

Reliable statistics regarding the total number of students currently involved in community action/service are difficult to obtain, partly because the term itself is not capable of precise definition and partly because few of the groups have formal constitutions and membership, their level of activity and support fluctuating rapidly over fairly short periods, not least as a result of the pressure of examinations on students' time towards the end of each academic year. But a survey of colleges in the Greater London area in 1971 revealed that a total of 1,500 students (out of an estimated total student population of 100,000) were actively engaged in some form of student community action during 1971–2 academic year, and that these were concentrated in 52 of the 240 colleges in Greater London.[9] The same survey revealed that London students were engaged in the different categories of community work in the following proportions:

20% Work with the elderly (cleaning, decorating, shopping, etc.)
18% Work with the homeless (including soup runs and other help for dossers and vagrants)
14% Work in schools (mostly groupwork for educationally handicapped children in 'inner city' schools)
9% Work with immigrants (especially English language tuition)
9% Work on adventure playgrounds
7% Work with playgroups (chiefly for children with single parents)
6% Work with youth clubs (including youth hostelling weekends for deprived teenagers)
4% Work in hospitals
3% Work with welfare rights stalls and neighbourhood advice centres
2% Work with young addicts
2% Work with the disabled (chiefly 'ferrying' to and from clubs, etc.)
6% Miscellaneous (including gypsy education, mentally handicapped or educationally subnormal children, young delinquents, community and tenants associations, and others)

Projected onto a national scale, these results would indicate a total involvement of perhaps 7,500 students – a poor total indeed by comparison with the American estimate of 400,000 mentioned earlier, and perhaps most conveniently compared with the average gate at a second or third division football match (a revealing measure of the true extent of social activism in Britain's student

population!). It would be misleading to project the relative per-
centages quoted in the table above onto a national scale as well,
since certain of these figures are biased by the particular patterns
of social need prevailing in the capital, not least the acute and
accelerating shortage of reasonably priced accommodation for single
people and low-income families. Thus the fact that nearly one-fifth
of the total were recorded as working with the homeless is a simple
measure of the particular incidence of this area of need within the
Greater London area. The same survey, analysed by types of
college, showed that a substantial majority of the students were
drawn from universities and that the colleges of education were also
well represented. But the polytechnics' showing was unimpressive
and colleges of all other kinds were barely represented at all. These
findings are not surprising – since SCA is so heavily dependent upon
the financial and other resources of student unions, it is natural
that it should flourish in those institutions whose unions are
strongest, and that it should have almost totally failed to take root
in, for example, colleges of further education which, as a rule, have
a high proportion of rather young (and/or part-time) students and
very weak student union organisation.

In considering the types of student activity themselves, it is
convenient to group them into four principal categories. Firstly,
there are those students who are working chiefly under the auspices
of agencies or organisations external to the higher education system,
and whose work is least influenced by the fact of their student status.
In London primary schools, for example, several head teachers
have welcomed students who are willing to commit themselves to
visiting at a regular period each week to assist with groupwork or
to give individual tuition to slow learners, and to help with such
activities as football for which these schools are not, as a rule,
well equipped or well staffed. There are similar contacts with youth
clubs in a number of areas, and one special category of project for
which students have shown themselves to have a particular aptitude
is the leadership of 'adventure weekends' for disadvantaged teenagers, under the auspices of the Youth Hostels Association. Playgroups have been started in several cities, with notably successful
examples in Bradford and York, while a small London theological
college now runs a playgroup specifically for the children of homeless families temporarily in the care of the local authority. In a
similar vein, adventure playgrounds are popular venues for student
work. The City University students' union was instrumental in

securing a site for the construction of a playground in Finsbury from Islington Borough Council, and in building the equipment in conjunction with local residents' associations. At Bristol Polytechnic, students from the faculty of art and design designed and constructed a playground at Farleigh Mental Hospital as a part of their third year course (see David Brockington's chapter in this book), and for two successive years a course has been run by the Imperial College community action group to train those students wishing to spend a part of their summer vacations working in the fast-proliferating field of holiday playschemes of all kinds. In conjunction with the Mobil Oil Company, the University of London Union sponsored the conversion of a disused lorry into a mobile playground, which was stationed on a number of East End sites, until eventually destroyed by arson. A number of colleges have organised holidays for children from deprived backgrounds. Hatfield Polytechnic made use of its field research centre as a summer camp for children from London slums, while Camberwell School of Art has arranged and supervised trips to the sea and the countryside for children in the care of the Southwark social services department. Clubs for educationally subnormal and mentally handicapped children have attracted student support in several places, and work with adult mental patients is taking place in Bristol, Nottingham (at Rampton Hospital) and elsewhere. The New College of Speech and Drama's students have provided drama therapy for members of a Camden club for the mentally ill.

Work with the elderly has conventionally taken the forms of visiting, cleaning, decorating and the like, a common pattern in most areas, but in Cardiff this has been extended to a survey to discover the awareness of old people of their entitlement to social benefits and welfare rights. Similar surveys in Salford, Birmingham and Bangor have been conducted to discover the extent of unmet needs among the disabled, for benefits from their respective local authorities, under the provisions of the Chronically Sick and Disabled Persons' Act. In Wandsworth and Haringey, students have been active in the running of welfare rights stalls, as a form of mobile, market-place citizens' advice bureaux, and Portsmouth Polytechnic has fostered links with a local claimants' and unemployed workers' union (likely, perhaps, to be the forerunner of many, as students find themselves forced to rely upon the largesse of the Supplementary Benefits Commission, as the level of students' grants falls progressively further behind the fast accelerating rise in the student cost-of-living index). A Birmingham group was centrally involved in organising a rent strike among tenants of the City Council in a particularly run-down neighbourhood and rather intermittent links with tenants' associations have been established elsewhere.[10] A number of colleges have participated in language tutoring projects (and, in the Borough of Ealing, 'Saturday schools') sponsored by local community relations councils, but the discontinuity of students' presence in their place of study has hampered the expansion of this particular category of work, since it is one in which continuity of personal contact on an individual basis is of particular importance. Hospital visiting is another sphere of conventional voluntary work to which students have not so far been attracted in large numbers, except in the rather special case of the Hospital for Sick Children at Great Ormond Street in London, which has proved to have a quite exceptional appeal. In Cambridge and some other cities, students have joined the volunteer staff of the Samaritans and in Nottingham they are involved in the setting up of a 'Niteline' telephone counselling service for young people in general. In Nottingham too there is a connection with the Probation Service, with student involvement in both the experimental scheme for Community Service Orders established by the Criminal Justice Act 1972 and in a local hostel for ex-Borstal boys.[11] Medical students from St Thomas's Hospital in London have been recruited to the Youth Resettlement Project, sponsored by the Probation Service, to befriend and help homeless and unemployed young ex-offenders.

New Horizon, Centrepoint and other centres providing temporary shelter for homeless young (usually single) people – in the case of New Horizon, particularly those with the additional problem of narcotic drug dependence – have attracted student support, as have a number of centres catering for older, single, homeless people, particularly alcoholics. London, Glasgow, Exeter, Hull, Portsmouth and Swansea students have all helped with the operation of regular nightly soup runs for dossers, and a number of hostels and night refuges use help of a similar kind. At Southampton and Cheltenham, students have been active in campaigns to oppose the closure of hostels for the homeless and both London and Cheltenham students have conducted surveys to refute statistics given in official reports, which have seriously underestimated the extent of need for welfare provision of this kind. Another socially isolated minority, that of the gypsies, has also received a substantial measure of student support. At Manchester University, the students' union's recreational and washing facilities were made available to the residents of a nearby gypsy encampment (predictably, provoking a measure of ill-concealed hostility from civic and academic dignitaries), while All Saints' College, Tottenham, has set up a caravan school at a temporary camp in Enfield. Students from a number of universities, among them Cambridge, have played an active part in both gypsy liaison groups and gypsy education programmes, and at Bristol they have been in the forefront of a campaign to persuade the local authority to accept its responsibility for providing permanent sites under the provisions of the 1968 Caravan Sites Act. At Bradford a group involved in setting up a community centre on an exceptionally isolated council estate gained student help, while at Uxbridge the students of Brunel University have inaugurated a series of annual community festivals under the title of Brunelzeebub, which have incorporated both 'open days' for the University and displays and performances by local schools, societies, and organisations of all kinds.[12]

A second principal category of projects consists of those in which efforts have been made to secure access by community organisations and groups to resources and facilities possessed by colleges themselves. This is far easier said than done, partly because of practical problems of security, insurance and the like, but equally because of the psychological barriers which appear to divide institutions of higher education generally from the community at large. Academics are, on the whole, remarkably unconcerned at events taking place beyond their institutional walls, but members of the wider community are all too often entirely ignorant of the nature and purpose of these institutions in their midst, and the resources they can offer. There are, of course, the long-established extra-mural programmes of all kinds, but these seldom relate directly to the immediate concerns of the locality, and represent, in any case, a wider sharing of only a university's or college's intellectual resources, when what local groups very often require is help of a far more mundane and practical kind. One such instance – that of the opening of Manchester's student union facilities to gypsies – has been quoted already. Another can be found at two South London colleges of education (Digby Stuart and Philippa Fawcett), each of which is situated in a district with a comparative poverty of recreational provision for children. The college premises have been opened to the children at weekends and facilities made available (under the

D

supervision of the students themselves) for creative drama, art, crafts, improvised games, etc. In many colleges, too, the sports fields represent a grossly under-used asset of a kind which is frequently lacking in the community at large. Some colleges have made their playing fields available for use by primary schools or youth clubs (though the Polytechnic of North London encountered an absolute and inexplicable veto by the Inner London Education Authority in its attempt to do likewise), while another (Birkbeck), has made its pavilion available to house a playgroup run on a co-operative basis by local mothers. Further examples of a similar kind are hard to discover, however – a surprising and sobering fact, when regard is had for the very considerable capital assets which universities and colleges possess. Not infrequently, local community groups founder for want of something as simple as the occasional use of a duplicator – here, surely, is assistance which no college, of whatever kind, would find it hard to offer?

Since the category of resource possessed most conspicuously by students is their academic knowledge, however, more importance ought perhaps to be attached to cases where they have sought to place this at the disposal of groups and individuals in the wider community. This is not an approach which is readily applicable in all cases – some disciplines can more easily be applied in a social context than others, and many students prefer to seek in community work a therapeutic relief from their studies, rather than a means of further applying them. But developments of this kind are fractionally more likely to enjoy the approval and even active support of college authorities, and may show further development, if current student interest in the concept of 'community-related curricula' bears fruit. One of the earliest and best publicised exercises of this kind was a survey conducted by Birmingham University medical students into the incidence of hypothermia among elderly residents of the city – the shock findings of which sparked off a major series of other forms of student community action among the elderly. At the London Hospital Medical College in Whitechapel, medical students have again been particularly active, in this case through conducting a wide-ranging inquiry into the medical needs of the area and into the views of local residents, doctors and other health workers, on current plans for National Health Service reorganisation. Students from the Guildhall School of Music and Drama have also been working in London's East End, by visiting primary schools to present programmes of improvised drama, encouraging full pupil-participation and the same schools have benefited from the interest of geographers at Queen Mary College in developing an awareness and understanding of the physical and social environment of Dockland, through practical investigations by pupils into its history, its present needs and future prospects. At the London School of Economics, lecturers and students within the law faculty have set up a welfare appeals service, to offer free legal advice and representation to claimants appearing before supplementary benefits and rent tribunals (at which statutory legal aid is not yet available). With the encouragement of the London Council of Social Service, London OSCA (a co-ordinating body for Student Community Action groups throughout the Greater London area) has established a 'language bank' or register of students fluent in less common foreign languages, who are willing to act as interpreters in situations of emergency, for example, in hospitals, police stations and at air and seaports. (It is noteworthy that this scheme has proved to be one of the very few through which significant numbers of overseas students have been attracted into community action.) At Chelsea College, a group of student pharmacists has been active in giving talks to teenagers in schools and youth clubs about the uses and abuses of hallucinogenic drugs, and members of the Architectural Association's school of architecture have served as advisers to a number of community groups engaged in opposing unsuitable local authority redevelopment plans – most notably in Covent Garden. Trainee teachers from Southlands College (as a part of their course) have offered literacy training to black teenagers in Brixton youth clubs, and others from Liverpool colleges were deeply involved in the work of the Liverpool Educational Priority Area team. Social science students (for example, those from the Polytechnic of North London) have been widely involved in the conducting of surveys, to discover deficiencies in the coverage of local authority welfare services. But the vast majority of these schemes have been conducted in an extra-syllabic if not extra-curricular context, with only a limited measure of interest or support from academic staff. The reply of the Professor of Greek at the Queen's University, Belfast, to a questionnaire circulated by the Education Secretary of the students' union is perhaps fairly typical of the attitude of many, even in less esoteric disciplines: 'You lay great emphasis on relevance. In my opinion, however, the concept of relevance is not one which, in all circumstances, is necessarily appropriate to an academic community engaged in the pursuit of learning. . . . We try to get at the truth in its infinite and often puzzling variety.'[13]

A final significant category of projects is that in which the desire for large-scale student involvement has been consciously rejected, in favour of much more selective intervention in specific localities and groups, solely in instances where such action may assist in the realisation of goals which would otherwise be difficult for the local community to obtain. This type of approach is much closer to the practice of professional community workers than of traditional volunteers in social work, and has so far been attempted in a significant and clearly-planned manner only in Cardiff, under the auspices of Cardiff Student Community Action (CSCA). This is a registered charity, whose offices are housed at the students' union of Cardiff University College and whose income is derived in part from student sources, but which is in other respects somewhat apart from the mainstream of student activism. CSCA has defined as its particular sphere of interest the depressed inner city residential area of Adamsdown, a locality with a poor physical stock of housing, a high unemployment rate and a conspicuous lack of recreational amenities, now threatened with partial destruction by an urban motorway scheme. Four principal projects have so far been launched. Firstly, they have headed efforts to set up a Neighbourhood Advice and Information Centre, housed in a disused shop and staffed by professionals – a youth and community worker, a receptionist and a part-time solicitor. This centre provides free information on legal matters of all kinds, offers practical facilities to local self-help organisations and pressure groups, and assists with initiating new services to help some of the area's many unmet needs. Secondly, they were in the forefront of a successful campaign to oppose the intention of the city and university authorities to create a large 'university precinct' (or ghetto) in central Cardiff, by destroying an area of working class housing (which also provided cheap accommodation for students) and compulsorily removing the inhabitants to isolated estates on the city's outskirts. This planning battle was, perhaps, a classic instance of the harnessing of students' social concern (and the use of their articulateness in argument and knowledge of planning law) to the service of a section of the community which, though seriously affected by the intentions of remote officialdom, would otherwise have been virtually powerless to resist the threats to its survival. Thirdly, CSCA was one of a number of groups instrumental in creating a Rights and Information Bureau

(RIB) to meet the needs of young people for information of a kind not normally available from such semi-official agencies as citizens' advice bureaux. Two full-time workers handle a constant flow of inquiries on such matters as bail, divorce, drugs and abortion. Fourthly, the group is now actively involved in converting a disused corner store into a neighbourhood children's centre, to be equipped with facilities for play, indoor games, arts, crafts, drama, a 'quiet room' for homework and the like.

CSCA has been notably successful in securing funds from both educational, public and charitable sources to make a programme on this scale possible, and few other colleges seem likely to emulate it for some time. Determined leadership, a clear definition of aims, and continuity of these over time are indispensable if effective community organising is to develop – and these are not qualities in which student organisations, by their very nature, are normally strong. So the future development of student community action is not easy to discern. A prolonged period of Conservative government at national level might one day – like the 1950s and early 1960s – cause the majority of socially aware and radical students to return to normal patterns of party political activism within the broad framework of the Labour Movement. A repetition of the 1964–70 experience of the Labour Party in office, on the other hand, might once again drive many of them out of the mainstream of organised politics in despair and in this situation the more radically charged manifestations of community action would certainly be strengthened. It is difficult to discover hard data on what happens to student community activists on graduating from student status, but subjective impressions suggest that many of those who were first exposed in this context to situations of real human need come in time to regard these as manifestations of an inequitable and oppressive social order, and move from a position of vague humanitarian goodwill to one of serious political commitment. Because of the ephemerality and endemic impecuniosity of students as a group, it seems fair to predict that the purely student-initiated extra-mural manifestations of student community action are likely to remain on a fairly modest scale. Certainly there is, at present, no sign of their being regarded with the degree of favour in official quarters (or of their attracting the consequent material and financial support) which their American counterparts enjoy. So, in the long run, the future of student community action as a whole will probably depend on developments in the curricular sphere. If patterns of community concern are built into courses at all levels, in institutions of all kinds, and the social application of knowledge comes to be regarded as an integral and normal part of the learning experience, then we may legitimately hope that our universities and colleges will become, in reality, resource centres upon which the entire community can draw. But such developments are unlikely to be realised until such time as the organised student union movement can be persuaded to turn its attention away from immediate material issues of accommodation or grants, at least in part, and to focus its sights instead on the academic establishment's central prerogative – to determine the content of the curriculum itself. To achieve change in this quarter, students must analyse where the true centres of power now lie – in individual departments and institutes and in the long-established tradition of professorial power. At departmental level, the student movement remains ill-organised and insecure, unsure of its aims and too easily intimidated by the threat of 'failure' wielded by the operators of the hierarchical system that obtains. But if student community activists are sincere in their intentions and claims, then it is here that their success will be registered. New principles of 'academic responsibility' will be defined, to replace the purely passive notions of 'academic freedom' which have prevailed until now, and the educational system will become both one in which the entire community can be involved, and one by which the entire community is served.

REFERENCES

1   *Quotations from Chairman Mao Tse-Tung*, Foreign Languages Press, Peking, 1966.
2   *Volunteering – A Manual for Students*, National Student Volunteer Program, Washington, 1971.
3   For a full account see E. P. Thompson (ed) *Warwick University Ltd – Industry Management and the Universities*, Penguin, Harmondsworth, 1970.
4   Joseph H. Blatchford 'Action Supports Student Volunteers' in *Synergist*, National Student Volunteer Program, Washington, Spring 1972.
5   'UYA Unites Academe with Action' (unsigned) in *Synergist*, National Student Volunteer Program, Washington, Spring 1972.
6   Ray Cashell 'Community Related Curricula' in *SCANUS Newsletter*, National Union of Students, London, January 1973.
7   Eric Midwinter *Priority Education – An Account of the Liverpool Project*, Penguin Education, Harmondsworth, 1972.
8   For a fuller discussion of these distinctions see Robert Holman

'Students and Community Action' in *Universities Quarterly*, Spring 1972.

9 *Annual Report 1972*, London Organisation for Student Community Action, London, 1972.

10 A detailed description of projects in Birmingham, plus a historical survey of the development of student social action in Britain generally, appears in Alan Barr *Student Community Action*, Bedford Square Press, London, 1972.

11 Richard Banyard 'News from Nottingham' in *SCANUS Newsletter*, National Union of Students, London, January 1973.

12 For a detailed list of student action projects in all parts of Britain (except London), classified by type of work, see *Student Community Action Kit*, National Union of Students, London, 1972. For a similar list in London, see *Annual Report 1972*, London Organisation for Student Community Action, London, 1972.

13 Ray Cashell 'Community Related Curricula' in *SCANUS Newsletter*, National Union of Students, London, January 1973.

Chapter Two

Student Help for the Educationally Disadvantaged

BY ERIC MIDWINTER

Eric Midwinter is Principal of the Liverpool Teachers' Centre and Head of the Liverpool Home School Development Unit. This grew out of *Priority*, a national centre in Liverpool for urban community education, which was itself a continuation and extension of the Liverpool Educational Priority Area Project of which he was the director from 1968 to 1971. He graduated in History from Cambridge University, took an M.A. in Education at Liverpool, and a Ph.D. at York University. He was a Co-Director of the Advisory Centre for Education, Cambridge, and acted as Educational Consultant to the Home Office Community Development Projects. His books include *Social Administration in Lancashire, 1830–1860*, 1969, *Victorian Social Reform*, 1968, *Nineteenth Century Education*, 1968, *Projections: An EPA Project at Work*, 1972,[1] *Social Environment and the Urban School*, 1972,[2] *Priority Education*, 1972[3] and *Patterns of Community Education*, 1973.

Having worked for over five years in projects designed to assist the socially and thus educationally disadvantaged child, one of the more optimistic notes to sound is the benefit of student help. The social injustices, indeed the social justices, of Educational Priority Areas, have been well-rehearsed. Districts of multiple deprivation, principally but not exclusively in the inner hearts of our cities and larger towns, provide a chilling obstacle to the educational development of the children in them. Poor housing, low income, inadequate services, harassed and broken families, an insecure and restless atmosphere; all the dread problems of the age assemble and multiply amid the rubble of destroyed homes and the gaunt horrors of highrise development. Equality of educational opportunity has a mocking ring in such places. One could shock and horrify with black anecdotes of children and parents crippled, socially and intellectually, by their circumstances, but the cold statistics are despairing enough for the least sensitive conscience. In so far as higher education is an indicator of the life-chances offered by our society, then a good suburban class of thirty children will normally see half a dozen through to higher education, whereas an EPA class would count itself lucky if even one made it. Even when the figures are not extreme, but merely stated as middle class versus working class, using the Registrar General's category, the picture is still one of gross inequality. It takes thirty-five sets of working-class parents to produce a higher education candidate; it takes only seven middle-class families to emulate them.

Hopefully, one need not, yet again, heavily belabour the case of educational inequality and parental privilege. Most people are aware of, perhaps ashamed of, the unfairness of the situation. From 1968 to 1971 the Government, spurred on by the Plowden Report which coined the designation, sponsored the National Educational Priority Area Projects, to carry out action-research with a view to recommending a national policy for such areas. Liverpool was one of the five areas chosen for this pioneer work and, along with others, we made our recommendations to the Department of Education and Science in the early spring of 1972. These proposals, under the heading of the Halsey Programme,[4] all follow the theme of community education, the idea that schooling and other educational provision should draw on the strength and repair the weaknesses of the community it serves. The six major recommendations pursue the major principles of community education – positive discrimination allied with local diagnosis, an intimate interrelation with all facets of community life and an awareness of contributing to the overall strategy of community renewal. They constitute a fully-fledged pattern of community education designed to give our socially disadvantaged children – the latterday Olivers – a fair deal. You can remember the six recommendations quickly by reference to OLIVER:

Organise Community Education Task-Forces
Links with the Home-Educational Visitors and Public Relations
  Grants
Install Pre-Schools of all kinds for all
Venture into new projects
Extend the EPA concept
Resources Centres and College Links for all Schools

Liverpool distinguished itself by staying in business. With the hospitable assistance of the Liverpool Education Authorities and an amalgam of other bodies and individuals, *Priority* was established. It became a national centre for urban community education. From the solid base of its Liverpool activities, *Priority* hoped to offer a 'window' for the nation onto the educational problems of the urban child. We hoped to rally the EPA and allied movements and provide a focus for attention on this, the most critical problem facing English education. Our goal was the extension of community education, the establishment of balance and harmony between school and community at all levels. We hoped thus to create a stable foundation for the child's education and, beyond that, to help the urban school to become an agency for improving and developing community life in our towns and cities.

For this present purpose, the critical recommendation and aspect of our activities must be student involvement, but it would have been misleading to plunge directly into that without outlining the context. For the initial purpose of student involvement must be seen in its interlock with everything else concerned with community education. It is not a thing in itself, but a closely connected part of a pattern.

Priority worked with forty of Liverpool's designated EPA schools, and some thirty of them enjoyed college attachments. This totals some three hundred students in a year, coming from six or seven colleges of education. All of them are preparing for teaching. Ilkley College has recently started a full-time, three-year 'community education' course; Edge Hill College, Ormskirk, operates a one-year in-service diploma course for teaching the socially disadvantaged; dozens of Coventry College students are in regular contact with the excellent community education programme fostered under the aegis of the Home Office Community Development Project in that city; Wentworth Castle College is conducting highly rewarding work with children in deprived districts of the West Riding; and so on. The list is a growing one. Briefly, the hypothesis runs as follows: if we need urban Community Schools, we need urban Community School-teachers; if we need urban Community Schools, we need urban Community Colleges, or at least, urban Community Portions of courses at colleges to equip them.

A major aphorism of community education is that schools do not attempt to reach or maintain a similiarity; rather should they differ according to communal needs and characteristics. There is an urgent job to be done in training professional teachers, eager, sensitive and inventive enough for so onerous a task. Too often we are told by teachers that they were not trained to familiarise themselves with disadvantaged social background . . . or to cope with pressing needs of particular communities . . . or to enter into dialogue with parents in socially deprived districts.

In creating what we called 'EPA option courses', it was our responsibility to go some way to close this yawning chasm between the vagaries of teacher-education and the realities of the downtown school. In so doing, we echoed a recommendation of the Plowden Report on primary schools; namely, that Colleges of Education should establish 'continuing links' with an EPA school or group of schools. It is interesting to recall why and how we started this idea, back in 1968. One of our ploys was to examine whether the normal primary school curriculum could be 'socialised', in an attempt to give it a 'community' orientation. For instance, by simulating a large supermarket as a maths base, one school was able to integrate with all manner of social and even moral aspects of the child's everyday life. We asked colleges to help by providing a task-force in each school, and this many of them did. It was a tiring exercise consummating these, at first, sometimes uneasy marriages; perhaps the most fatiguing work we did. There is a long and not by any means unreasonable suspicion of colleges in schools, whilst sometimes the colleges were a little brash in their approach. Certainly there were many administrative snags in the opening year and it is as well to remember that Rome wasn't built in a day and, even then, it wasn't student labour that was deployed. Assuredly our relatively long-term phasing was important. So many projects and so on are for the nonce, with a group of students available for a term or a year and then, bingo, they vanish.

We are talking about steadfast, ongoing linkages between institutions: the students and sometimes the teachers change, but the college-school link is solid. There is, I believe, a lesson here for higher education's attempts to engage in communal and other activities. A continuing service is the only way to ensure eventual success and is the only fair approach to the clientele. Our view is that it took nearly three years to pioneer the liaison with eleven schools before we were able to transfer the idea to eighteen or so others. Remember, too, that we are talking about agencies scarcely foreign to one another: indeed, few higher education agencies would be in a position to deal so directly with a body as close in character as colleges are to schools.

Both the 'how' and the 'why' were inevitably changed as the experiment grew. Although the social environmental syllabus remained – and does remain – at the core of the work, the exercise itself soon overwhelmed the content of the exercise. It was the link-up in itself which became most meaningful. Teachers reported that the children were benefiting from the sheer luxury of their own adult (and an almost qualified adult, at that) to talk with for a day. Mothers told me of children leaving home earlier on the 'student' day to meet 'their' student when he or she arrived. Teachers told me of hearing, for the first time in their careers, students talk of 'our' school. It became a two-way adventure. Students responded to their hospitable reception in the schools by inviting the children back to the college. This spread to children and their parents. Film shows, galas, pantomimes were laid on; college facilities were opened up and these were like a magical treasure trove to the children; tea with your student in his or her bed-study room was an especial treat. It was once my delight to watch students and children wandering hand in hand through the college, critically examining the work on the area around the college which they had done together.

The normal procedure was for a team of eight to twelve students to visit the school optimally for a day each week. Usually they associated themselves with a particular class in the school, while also acting in a general helpmeet capacity to the school at large, going to school camp, helping at sports days, open days, Christmas functions, school entertainments and so forth. The tutor and class teacher between them organised the operation for the term or the year, with, according to personality and temperament, one or other usually taking a lead. They were at the apex of the pyramid and, like pope and emperor in the far-off days of the Holy Roman Empire, tutor and teacher often appeared to share the functions of mitre and sword to the children. To sustain the medieval metaphor, the student group were like the barons, each, in turn, with his or her group of three or four children as (according to one's view on pupil-power) the knights or serfs. For example, a close examination of the local shops led to each student-child team, under the overall direction of tutor and teacher, developing a special study of one type of shop. This led to the construction in the school of a huge shopping precinct, with each little troupe establishing its café, chip shop, corner shop and so on. When all was ready, the parents were invited in to enjoy the refreshments provided by the children in the 'Sunshine Café' and to buy items the children had made or grown.

The yearly continuation of all this activity, now in its fifth year, has led to a colourful and extensive outcrop of curricular materials. Language and social studies kits have been developed, and certain portions of the work have been modified for national publication. Now students and tutors are looking more keenly at the all-important home-school relations field, helping with exhibitions and magazines, and trying their hand at home visits and house-to-house surveys. This is, as many teachers now complain, a much neglected aspect of college training and there are, at present, signs of this being remedied. Other students are assisting in our pre-school endeavours (we underpin a federation of some thirty pre-school playgroups) including some interesting one-to-one correspondence action actually in the homes. At the adult level (we organise a score or so adult community education groups) specialist students have helped with keep-fit, low-budget cookery and other modes of tuition.

We asked for three guarantees. In the first place, the contact had to be regular, time-tabled and continuous. Although mostly the students are volunteers, we had to overcome, in the first year, the *ad hoc*, random appearances of students in their spare time. Of course, students return to the school in their leisure time *as well as* at the appointed hours and that is welcome. In the second place, we asked for a tutor-led team, with the group of students in constant receipt of tutorial assistance. In the third place, it was necessary to place the attachment in the context of a course. Ideally, as, for instance, at Liverpool's Notre Dame College, the unit is completed. Here five tutors lead five teams of second-year students in five schools, and they also mount the in-college education work for these students. Thus, principles can be drawn from and illustrated by the practical work which, in turn, can be refreshed by the intramural studies. Naturally, there is variety from college to college; some, for example, use third-year and others second-year students – never first-year students. It's deemed important to give them a chance of looking around before opting.

Practically all the teachers involved view the 'continuing link' as the most successful aspect of our work in Liverpool and, remembering the fatigue of initiating the scheme, that is wonderfully heartening. There seems, in fact, to be a six-fold benefit:

1 The children benefit from the variety and intensity of their studies made possible by a student team. The simple business of taking out children, for environmental studies and so on, is an obvious illustration. They form a sound relationship and they have what the teachers call 'conversation with an adult' for a day. All reports suggest the children grow in confidence, vocabulary and other socially fruitful features.

2 The students benefit from a realistic involvement with the problems many of them will come to face, and this they welcome. It also gives them a long-term chance to develop a relationship with three or four children and yet one not so intimate as to cause too much grieving at the end of the year on either side when, as the song says, the best of friends must part. It allows students to experiment with differing curricular ideas and we are always at pains to ensure that they see the role as part of the much grander strategy of a city-wide project with national ramifications. We have annually run a Liverpool intercollegiate conference and we have organised a national intercollegiate conference of EPA Option students with some twenty practical 'workshops'.

3 The teachers benefit from the sheer labour made available, from the scope it gives them to attempt extensive experimentation, and from the morale-boosting effects of being so closely involved with teacher-education. One or two have, naturally, been a little bothered by the incursion of student teams, but most welcome them avidly. The chief point is for the plan of campaign to be firm but flexible. Everyone, but most of all the teacher, needs to know where he stands. The teacher has the occasionally alarming task of having to sustain the activities during the week. We take great care to ensure that the 'student-day' is not a one-off bonanza, but is the session when the normal school process receives a boost. This is probably the subtlest and trickiest piece of classroom administration.

4 The tutor benefits from the comparison of theory and practice. In turn, he develops a rapport with his students and is seen by them much more as a fellow-worker. The sudden evaluations of the block school practice, with the tutor often feared as the dread evaluator, is replaced by a more urbane, leisurely repairing of weaknesses and reinforcing of strengths. The tutors' hardest task is in producing a co-ordinated body of theory from the diffuse elements of the practical situation. As many of them freely admit, what they call 'the old one-two' of the strictly hierarchical series of abstract lectures is a much easier option. It is, incidentally, most annoying that, just as some colleges are managing to bring practice and theory into a valid and proper conjunction (and this, as colleges are realising, is not just applicable in the EPA context) along comes the James Report. In defeatist style, with its estranged theoretical and practical cycles, it seems to have thrown in the towel and resigned itself to a non-alignment of the two elements.

5 The school benefits from the constant nurture of the college, which acts almost as a kind of resources centre and emergency service for the school.

6 The college benefits from its perpetually salutary reminder of the coalface of education, and from its opportunity to maintain close contact with educational reality.

One must reiterate the refrain of benefit. It is important that everyone and everything should benefit from such exercises. If such a programme can (as, ideally, we have shown it can) be of mutual value all round, then most problems fade. It is when one or other party is being 'used', to employ the word we have come most to fear, that troubles arise; or, and the distinction is small, when one or other party *thinks* it is being 'used'. And rightly so. There is no need for any dimension of educational whoredom on any side. The children must not be 'used' purely for the further-ment of student research; the students must not be 'used' merely as coolies for the teacher and the school; the teacher must not be 'used' as an inexpensive tutor substitute; the tutor must not be 'used' as a free, extra teacher-chauffeur-labour agent; the school must not be 'used' for tutors and students to assuage their guilt feelings about poverty; the college must not be 'used' as a dumping-ground cum gratis educational supermarket.

It is in the grand complex of mutuality that the aim is best achieved and the difficulties overcome. Even the children can be 'users', craftily playing off students' ends against teacher middles, dodging responsibility around inexperienced students and generally, as they say in show-business, 'taking five'. I recall years ago a student-led pupil crocodile wending through the streets: 'Hallo, mum,' cried one youngster to his mum admiring him from the doorstep, 'the stewdies are here; we can do what we like!'

Yet it is not a sentimental mutuality. This is not do-goodery: it is a directly professional enterprise. Occasionally, students do preen themselves as latter-day Lady Bountifuls, pouring out doles of educative charity to the deserving poor. This does not mean that these attachments are not joyful and affectionate: it means that we are ever eager to erase what a colleague called 'the pease-pudding mentality'. We soon found that this has not much to do with a student's age, class background, education and the rest. It is much more personalised than that. Condescension is as likely from the young, working-class lad as genuine engagement from the middle-aged, middle-class lady.

Now, sixteen students in a school of some two hundred children and ten staff may look, superficially, like an imposition, even for only a day or week. To take, as a concrete example, such a weekly happening in a school in downtown Liverpool, it resolves itself into a question of careful organisation. Two students, training for infant work, work with groups of fives-to-sevens, thereby reliev-ing one or two infant teachers to do some home visiting, getting to know mothers and helping them with their problems. Two students have taken responsibility for the school magazine. This is a properly printed affair – it has long been our advice that material going to homes should be of high-class production. The children provide the creative and documentary material, much of it based on studies of their own environment, and thus a tidy circle is developed, of children drawing on the 'community' for their sources, screening these for the school magazine and then sending the magazine back into the community. Two students assist with the mothers' club, a weekly get-together to discuss issues or engage in some recreational or practical activity, and a valuable chance for the students to glean insights into parental attitudes. Two students lead a group of children in nursing the school garden, which was, in fact, a derelict piece of land by the school, reclaimed as a 'site-improvement' scheme as part of the original EPA Project. This opens up very wide vistas. A chief element in the project was this idea of children fighting back against the dreariness of their surroundings, with positive and colourful 'site-improvement' schemes in and around the schools. Students have been of great value in assisting with such programmes, which include reclaimed gardens (including a fine roof garden on top of the school), extensive play-ground wall-murals, which have attracted much attention and delight, and anti-litter campaigns.

The other eight students are attached to one or two classes. Here the theme is leisure pursuits, not the least abrasive problem in the urban context, with underemployment and other factors having their effect. Drawing on their own hobbies and interests, eight students are able to offer a shopminder to children, in terms of leisure possibilities. Over a day, some students offer two options and, over a year, children might indulge in tasting two or more of such options. Over a four year cycle, all the junior children can enjoy the benefit of this kind of opportunity, underlining the strong case for continuity. Obviously, the range of interests on offer from eight students against one teacher is most impressive, to say nothing of the specialist treatment in those interests for perhaps only five or six children at one time. The pursuits range from fishing and dress-making to photography and tennis – the interests tend, of course, to be those within the range of the child growing up in the city, but who may, without this stimulus, be unaware of the type of activity suggested or, more especially, how and where to get involved. It is the very 'ordinariness' of this approach which is attractive, for every student, however diffident about social action, must surely have an interest or hobby to enthuse over with a group of youngsters.

At another school, on the other side of the city, the pattern is different. A group of twelve students split up, two to a class. They are extra pairs of hands for the teacher, and that, of itself, is splendid. But it is interesting to note the types of activity which the classes are engaged in and which, without students, could be less productive. One class may be developing a survey of the immediate locale or the history of a particular nearby street. A couple of history or geography students are very useful for escorting the children on their expeditions, as well as for helping digest and present findings back at the school base. Another class may be mainly responsible for the animal room in the school - another project, already ongoing in the school and sponsored by the EPA Project, in a highrise area where domestic pets are not normally permitted – and a pair of biology students could be of sound assistance in this regard. Another class might be involved in the school's own radio station and a student or two with special interests in the media could become involved in the interviewing, taping and other forms of preparation. Yet another class might be associated with the old age pensioners' group, which meets at the school and which provides a wonderful source of mutual activity for old and young. A history lesson, a 'broadcasting' session or an art and craft workshop takes on an entirely different climate when senior and junior citizens are sharing it, and students can help and learn from that kind of situation, so rarely found in the primary

E

school. As at the first school, a particular class might have some responsibility for the school magazine and, once more, there is a chance for student engagement. There is a pre-school group, mainly run by the mothers in the school, and the mothers themselves – some of whom, incidentally, assist with the care of the animals – have their own dressmaking classes and other activities, in the specially furnished parent room. These activities are supervised by the teachers and, yet again, there is a rare chance for students to align themselves with this sort of work.

One of the most notable features of this school is its exhibitions of work in local shops, pubs, betting shops and doctors' surgeries. This reaching out of the school into the natural focal haunts of the community is of the essence in community schooling. It is doubtful whether it could have progressed so extensively and been sustained so intensively without student assistance. Over a whole range of shops and other agencies, there is a weekly change of beautifully presented exhibits of children's work, complete, where necessary, with captions, all aimed at explaining to the locality what the substance and objectives of the school really are. To cap this brief case-study, several students – and this is true of several schools – join the school at its annual educational camp, providing much-needed assistance to teachers and children and themselves culling benefit from the sheer experience of living for a week with the children they have been teaching throughout the year.

I am hopeful that these two short descriptions of actual cases may go some way to illustrate the practical possibilities of students in schools. Needless to say, the kind of 'community school' exemplified in these two samples is all too rare. It also goes without saying, that these particular groups of students were very fortunate to find schools with such an exhilarating variety of items in which they might get themselves thoroughly experienced. But, in part, it operates in reverse. Schools can only proceed through those arduous pioneer phases of a community-based exercise, when the going is rough and necessarily strewn with early errors, if there exists some leeway for them to experiment. A portion of this 'slack', as we are wont to term it, has been and can be provided increasingly by students.

Certainly our major obstacles were of an administrative nature. Like other higher educational institutions, colleges of education develop by accretion rather than replacement. If EPA Options were to be established, they had somehow to be imposed on an existing structure. Our tutor liaison committee sweated blood over timetabling and certificate requirements, when it might better have been employed discussing the vital array of curricular activities which their students and they were producing. In turn, this sometimes made for student stress, as other tutors brought pressure to bear, or as the students themselves worried about not doing the 'same' studies as their comrades. When I compare the unmitigated chaos of the first year with the smooth character of the fifth, I am encouraged. What is obvious is that it requires a total dedication and commitment on the part of the institution. What is also obvious is that, by a constant insistence on this high level of participation, one separates the men from the boys.

It is interesting to observe the students' own reactions. We take soundings whenever we can and, in the second year, the response of eighty students might be summarised as follows.

Apart from its general pay-off in terms of training, sixty of these students were using these attachments directly in terms of their certificate courses, either in lieu of a school practice or as the basis for special studies in child development and the like. Given the administrative troubles mentioned earlier, this was an excellent proportion of students whose attachment had successfully been grafted onto the main body of collegiate work.

Asked what benefits students thought had accrued to children, there was an overwhelming response in terms of their improvement under constant individual attention from, as one student put, an adult 'other than teacher, friend or parent'. Sixty-two students made this point firmly. Thirty-seven students claimed that the novel width and variety of ideas and interests which a student team could assemble had made for a brighter awareness and a build-up of confidence in the pupils. Twenty mentioned the benefits of working together as a well-constructed group, while twenty-four specifically suggested that language, written and oral, had shown definite improvement. Two quotes seem to summarise this overall regard for the merit of individual attention: 'Through this social contact, language has developed and children have become more confident in expressing themselves, they are now prepared to make more decisions for themselves, they have a new awareness of their environment and there has been an arousing of their curiosity.' Or again: 'A withdrawn child now speaks spontaneously – a quiet child participates in all activities – an "over-active" child begins to become socially aware of her fellow-pupils.' There were respectable and proper notes of warning. Eleven students felt there had been some disruption for the children, with some 'over-excited', others grown 'over-dependent' and others thinking it 'a scive'. Six found it difficult to judge at all, beyond one who said the children looked on them as 'aunties'. Two said categorically that there had been no educational benefit for the children. No one is more aware than the project officers of how cautiously this testimony must be treated, how difficult it is, for instance, for a student to differentiate between his or her influence over a year and the school's and, indeed, society's influence. Nevertheless, sixty-two out of eighty were reasonably convinced that, through the weekly support they could give four to eight children, the children had shown evident social and educational improvement. Leaving aside the doubts about the students' self-analysing, perhaps it is not to naive to find pleasure in sixty-two students so eager and keen after their engagement with the EPA schools.

Turning to a harder area, that of student benefit, the reactions were rather more varied and, insofar as the questions were direct 'consumer' ones, self-appraisal is probably a useful guide. Asked about the pros and cons of EPA attachment, as opposed to 'block' practice and general educational studies, a number of issues were raised. Fifty students subscribed sturdily to the viewpoint that the weekly meeting was immensely helpful; it was less artificial; one could attack with renewed vigour each week; it was more realistic; theory and practice combined more easily; one could observe development and progress slowly and thoughtfully. Seventeen mentioned how vital the experience had been in learning of the EPA environment and its problems. Twenty-one saw it as an opportunity to experiment gradually, without the pressure of normal teaching-practice, and to enjoy the camaraderie of working in a team. A few found tutors 'more enthusiastic' under this regime and seventeen (all of whom had been on half-day attachment) pressed the case for two sessions or a full day. In this they confirmed the school view that anything less was inadequate.

There were some clashes of view. Two each found discipline harder or easier; four found preparation simpler with a week-by-week commitment, whilst eight had grave difficulties in terms of preparation and the interference with their other college work; three each found the variety of approach afforded by this term of attachment happily wide and unhappily narrow. These smaller figures obviously reflected particular situations but, these apart, there was an interestingly cross-sectioned spread of opinion. This applied to the anti- as well as the pro-brigade. Twenty-one felt there was 'a lack of continuous communication' with a weekly attachment and phrases like 'too many cooks', 'too many groups' and 'breaks the school routine' were employed. Eleven voted strongly for a 'block practice' as well as, or instead of, this mode of training. (This seems reasonable. The EPA Courses were suggested as a one-year option, with this kind of attachment complementing two or three 'block' practices.) Broadly speaking, the advantages and disadvantages listed make it difficult to draw a distinct line for and against, except to say that the main tenor of opinion was favourable and that students felt they had benefited from the attachment. Again, with students never the friendliest critics of the *alma mater*, this was encouraging.

A few random quotations may fill out the picture. It was 'much more interesting and worthwhile' work; children 'have time to get to know you' (a neat counterpoint to the more traditional comments of students getting to know children); it meant 'contact kept with schools – which is what our course is all about'; it allowed one to develop 'a friend to friend relationship'. Contrarily, it 'militated against a continuous theme'; it meant 'work rushed to get a visible result'; there was 'persistent scratching of the surface'; it was 'a highly depressing' enterprise without 'another means of escape'. Again, there was this curious split between those who found a week-by-week attachment more 'continuous' than a 'block' practice. This probably reflected all kinds of personal interactions; student preparation and approach; teacher assistance and sustenance of the work; tutor direction and college organisation, to name but a few. Certainly, given favourable conditions apropos these factors, there was and is not, *per se*, a reason why continuity is not possible. Indeed, in terms of child and student-teacher development, it should, normally, be more rewarding precisely because of its longer-term duration.

The students were asked in what way the EPA Option Courses had helped fit them for possible work in EPA schools. Seventy-three had found definite advantages, compared with seven who felt, on balance, they had had no specific coursework to assist them or had not gained from the coursework offered. Once more, this was a very high rate of approval, even granting that many students, having volunteered for these courses, might have been pre-disposed toward them. (For most students, they were 'options' in the sense that they had to opt for this or an alternative.) Most of the self-analysis of benefits gleaned revolved around changed attitudes. There was much more talk of 'insight' and 'awareness' of, for example, 'text-book problems'; 'I would now adopt a totally different attitude' claimed one student; 'a real eye-opener' was another heartfelt comment; it helped 'by making me make a relationship' said another; one had, said a fourth student, 'to fight the frustration and despair in oneself'; each child became, for a fifth, 'a personality' not 'a recipient for knowledge'; 'middle-class ideas cannot be applied' gloomily concluded another. Others spoke of the 'vitality and great character of the children'; they were 'children, only more so'; 'let the children' said one student, 'feel important – they are'; 'EPA children', claimed another student, 'are just as good as any other children', and so on. Throughout the replies to this query, the tone was clear and set, if, at times, understandably innocent. There was an ever-mounting awareness of the potential of the children, the problems of their parental and social backgrounds and the limitations and difficulties imposed on the teacher. Several saw the advantage negatively; they had learned the hard way what the problem was; they had not yet discovered an answer.

There was a space for general comments and these reinforced the salutary nature of the exercise: 'Quite a surprising and enlightening experience'; 'an invaluable experience'; 'I often doubted myself'; 'I expected warmth – warmth was something I have to earn not expect'; 'fully justified and of mutual benefit'; 'the staff were a tremendous help'; 'thought-provoking' – these were some of the comments. Others merely reiterated earlier criticism both for and against. The 'social interaction' of the group approach was again referred to several times, as was the point that some felt the attachment 'a burden' because of its lengthiness. Twenty-eight spoke up enthusiastically for the EPA Option Courses in this general section, whereas eighteen voiced some criticism, usually along the lines of feeling their work spoilt somewhat by 'interference' from school or college staffs. Two of these only objected strongly to locality-based studies and parental involvement, and the criticisms chiefly were internal ones, suggesting ways of improving the enterprise, not advising its abolition. In a marvellous phrase, one student spoke of the danger of inflicting 'boring kindness' on the children.

The crunch question was: 'Is it your probable intention to teach in an EPA school?' There was a total of seventy-eight replies. These included one destined for secondary teaching, eleven 'don't knows', thirteen who were keen on EPA teaching, but were likely to be unlucky because of where they expected to live, thirteen straight negatives, eleven who expected to take up EPA teaching after gaining initial probationary experience elsewhere and twenty-nine definite positives. Of these twenty-nine, one admitted it had 'never been my intention', one added 'very much' to the 'yes' and one said 'for a period', after which she expected to be 'physically exhausted'. A probable intention of forty or just over 50 per cent of the replies was pleasing and the Liverpool LEA have notified us of student applicants who are specifically asking for EPA schools. Some might think the thirteen, who have, with the help of the EPA Option Courses, fervently decided against EPA schools are just as much a justification for the process as the forty who hope to join EPA staffs. The interesting division between those thinking of moving direct into EPA schools and those sanguine enough to consider fishing first in quieter waters recalls an on-going discussion in the area. There are teachers and tutors who strongly affirm that probationers should not directly move to EPA schools because of the toughness of the problems. Against that, personal suitability for EPA teaching is not just a matter of experience and it would be a pity if eminently-suited young teachers were lost for a year. Common sense suggests that no bold line need or should be taken, and that it is a highly individualised decision, as our breakdown of twenty-nine and eleven indicates.

The success has been splendid. I hope the minor pitfalls and the tests of endurance along the route have been duly noted. Let me reiterate that if colleges of education and schools can't find a working plan, then it's heaven help classics students hoping to involve themselves in, say, community law and order. The lessons can be simply stated: give it time to mature; let it be mutually valuable; attain a combination of theory and practice; ensure a steadfast professionalism; obtain complete commitment. Is it possible with other departments of other institutions, in other aspects of community development and action? Yes, it is possible: it may even be essential. A more crucial question is: is it likely? It's difficult, with all the will in the world, to be euphoric. Some universities are EPA landlords and some of the very conditions we need to combat are a direct consequence of university building programmes. In attitude and structure, some of the universities could be a thousand miles from the districts of urban blight. Some would argue it might be better if they were. I have become a trifle bitter about the lack of commitment in higher education to the urban crisis. It's partly an aloofness, most obvious in adding to the injury of destroying homes to build marvellous facilities, the injury of not letting anyone else use them, even in vacations. It's partly the outmoded structure, with certain of the departments unable, as they stand, to relate relevantly to the problems of the outside world. It's partly the 'academic respectability' bit, the shudders and grimaces which appear when the chance of utilitarian social effort presents itself. It's partly the unreliability (I speak with feeling) of agencies where people are always disappearing on holiday, or worrying about promotion and examinations, or being distracted by another fashionable crisis.

It must sound vaguely Chinese, but I would, if pushed, go to the extreme of suggesting that every higher education department should include a positive interflow with social action and utility, as part of the exercise of its particular discipline. Put in reverse fashion, should a higher education department, which can't, or won't, be granted exchequer succour? Eventually one hopes that the whole departmental structure will alter, as it already has in many primary and some secondary schools, and that departments or, preferably, inter-departments based firmly in the realities of everyday life and needs, will develop. Until the Arcadian time when the community university or college takes its place alongside the community school, when, in fact, all those vested academic interests are overcome, we must perforce strain and twist to sustain the grassroots movements.

The use of law and medical students in neighbourhood advice or health centres is clear enough, at least in concept. Technology and engineering put to the service of solving the technical troubles of highrise life or pre-school play provision is equally simple. Planners and architects and the like have tasks to perform of helping in the participation processes and even in the harder task of actually constructing and maintaining. The social sciences are another obvious series of reserve strengths for communities. The sciences can assist – there should be testing of foodstuffs and watchings over pollution and even a service and production role to play. The humanities are something of a difficulty and paradoxically so, in that the artist, the writer, the moralist and the historian have always been to the fore in exposing injustice and campaigning for reform. Maybe they should keep up this good work and localise it. Maybe they should be at the community's shoulder, helping it to phrase its argument, depict its woes and demand its rights. There are facile, but not silly, possibilities, like historians learning from the old as they help them, or geographers learning from community transport as they operate it. Basically, I do not believe that any higher education source worth its salt and name could not, with thought and devotion, find appropriate ventures in social action. I am also convinced that, with such an injection, many courses would be more stimulating, intellectually and culturally, than they presently are, for so many are sterile, sad and dry.

Yet it is imperative that, in one sense, the academic tradition is religiously maintained. This must all be seen as a step towards an interactive society, where the university is as much part and parcel of day to day life as the factory or the shop, and where bus conductors no longer shout 'Butlin's' to warn passengers that the next stop is nearest the university. It is not a case of students flexing their frail revolutionary muscles as, earnestly and vainly, they attempt to whip up pseudo-leftist fervour among the poor. This attitude is no less patronising than the 'pease-pudding mentality'. Our student activities have been most successful where students have, in an admirable harmony of the dispassionate and the compassionate, offered their academic or professional skills to the community, and have, conversely, evinced genuine appreciation for the opportunity afforded them of testing such skills against a real challenge. In that the traditions of higher education sustain that stance, they should be preserved.

In this regard, the higher education institutions portray the antithesis of the Pauline dilemma. They are reservoirs bursting with talent and resources, which are rarely placed at the public's disposal. The flesh is strong, but the spirit is unwilling.

REFERENCES

1 Eric Midwinter, *Projections: An EPA Project at Work*, Ward Lock Educational, London, 1972.
2 Eric Midwinter, *Social Environment and the Urban School*, Ward Lock Educational, London, 1972.
3 Eric Midwinter, *Priority Education*, Penguin, Harmondsworth, 1972.
4 A. H. Halsey, *Educational Priority*, vol 1, HMSO, London, 1972.

Chapter Three

The Student of Literature and the Needs of Children

BY GEOFFREY SUMMERFIELD

Geoffrey Summerfield is Senior Lecturer in the Departments of Education and English at the University of York. He was educated at Queen Mary College, London University, and at the University of Birmingham. He has taught at High School and at Teachers' College and has been visiting professor at the University of Nebraska (1968–9), Ontario Institute for Studies in Education (1971), and the University of California, Berkeley (1971–2). His books include *Topics in English*, 1965, *Look What I've Made*, 1972, and *The Creative Word*, 1972. He has also edited numerous books, including *The Later Poems of John Clare* (with E. Robinson), 1964, *Creativity in English*, 1967, *Voices, An Anthology of Poetry and Art*, 1968, *Matthew Arnold and the Education of the New Order* (with P. Smith), 1969, *Junior Voices, An Anthology of Poetry and Art*, 1970, *Creatures Moving*, 1970, *English in Practice* (with S. Tunnicliffe), 1971, and *First Voices*, 1971.

> 'Perhaps it was because teaching came naturally to Mr Stelling, that he set about it with that uniformity of method and independence of circumstances, which distinguish the actions of animals understood to be under the immediate teaching of nature.'
>
> GEORGE ELIOT, *The Mill on the Floss*

> 'Nature is made better by no mean
> But Nature makes that mean.'
>
> SHAKESPEARE, *The Winter's Tale*

The study of literature appears, superficially, to be in a healthy condition: the great seams of ore – Shakespeare, Milton, Wordsworth *et al.* – appear to be well nigh inexhaustible and the bibliographies of scholarly studies grow apace. New universities spring up with new departments of Eng. lit. which burgeon, flourish and develop an impressive panoply of post-graduate studies. The limits of legitimate fields of study are slowly extended: James Joyce, for example, who was distinctly peripheral twenty years ago, is now providing work for many graduate students. The story is a familiar one: it has to do with death. Senior professors retire to die, and yesterday's apprentices acquire the power and status to make policy. Empires fall, yielding place to new ones, and shifts in curriculum are to be observed everywhere.

But many students of literature – the persons in whose name, and for whose enlightenment, such proliferations and accretions take place – many are, I suspect, in a state of crisis. This is not to deny that, in the foreseeable future, it's likely that students will, for the most part, continue to apply themselves to the study of literature; nor to deny that most of them will continue to appear to acquire many of the skills and convictions, the insights and prejudices of their tutors. Nor is it to deny that it is still possible to believe that literature is an important part of the dominant culture of Western society, both in the sense that it offers a way in which we try to understand 'where we have been' and in the sense that a current literature is one crucial way of achieving an appropriately complex, subtle and responsive sense of 'where', at the moment, we are. (Though it's clear that if contemporary writers were dependent on official university patronage, they would be living on bread and water.)

Literature is clearly here to stay, and so is the institutionalised study of literature. The issue lies elsewhere, in the morale and sense of purpose of the student. The talented student of literature, as distinct from he who uncritically toes a line and minds the Ps and Qs, is not entirely happy with what he is doing. It is not that the syllabus is inherently uncongenial, for most departments of English have begun to tolerate some degree of choice in this matter; it is, rather, that the rationale, the *raison d'être*, of the activity itself is in doubt. And if the undergraduate student experiences qualms and misgivings, the student-teacher senses them much more acutely and urgently.

My own professional responsibility is not only with undergraduate students of English and the odd graduate who unwittingly drifts into my area of special competence, but also with English graduates who themselves propose to teach English. I propose, in this essay, to attend to these last, not only because they are at a very puzzling stage in their own development, but also because they represent the means whereby university English departments and their assumptions and orthodoxies feed back into the 'mainstream'.

These graduates have just given three years to the study of literature. Their 'brightest' peers are probably doing graduate work in English – an M.A. on Wordsworth or a Ph.D. on necrophilia in seventeenth-century poetry – and the student-teacher has a rather uneasy suspicion that he himself is moving toward the teaching-of-English-in-school *faute de mieux*; that, if he were really good, he would, like his betters, be delving among metaphysical bones. Again, he is uncertain and perplexed because his own roles are changing; he is now being asked to design a curriculum rather than exercise limited options within someone else's curriculum; he is about to 'give' rather than receive. (I argue not that this is necessarily a correct perception of his condition but that it *is his* perception, insofar as it is explicitly formulated.)

His natural reaction to this chrysaloid state is this: he prepares to arm himself. He, naturally enough, does this by attending to the 'art of teaching' rather than to the act of learning. And he does it, furthermore, by conceiving of his teaching role as that of mediator, explicator, examiner and critic. In brief, he conceives of literature as something with which the teacher 'does' something and he construes this 'doing' as the crucial matter, the nub of his professional competence. Insofar as he is able or willing to consider the data, the objects of his doing, he will probably concede that, yes, in school as distinct from university, there should probably be more room for modern literature; that, yes, there may not be much room for Anglo-Saxon homilies or the more obscure Middle English poems. But, short of a decisively radical jolt, he is not prepared to concede much more. And this, despite the fact that he may not feel at all happy about his own fairly recent experience of English *in school*.

The university has endorsed certain ways of proceeding, and a certain body of material with which to proceed. And the weight of this endorsement is fairly heavy. The influence of this endorsement is, moreover, retroactive: it bears directly on the schools. It is, for example, no accident that, as I write, many sixth-formers – kids of seventeen – are studying Book One of Wordsworth's *Prelude*. I happen to believe that *The Prelude* has been one of the most important reading events of my life, and it is precisely for this reason that I find the notion of seventeen-year-olds studying the poem, or part of it, to be grossly indecorous. Justifications for its inclusion in a lower sixth curriculum are, of course, legion: the poem is 'difficult', that is, it demands and merits strenuous intellectual exertion; it is a 'great' poem, therefore a requisite part of a respectable literature curriculum; its study is a prototype of subsequent study of literature at university; it is a poem that sixth form teachers presumably enjoy teaching. . . . One could go on at great length. But with the best will in the world, I consider its study by seventeen-year-olds to be a grotesque experiential aberration. Not because it is a poem that looks back, and sifts and appraises earlier experiences (such backward-glancing introspection is, of course, a 'natural' part of late adolescence in our own dislocating culture), and not because it *is* a difficult poem, though one shudders to think of the presumptuous cleverness with which some high achievers of seventeen will insist on 'understanding' it. No, my objection is, rather, this: that the kind of reappraisal, of critical reflection, that one finds in *The Prelude* is not a useful or profitable activity for adolescents who are themselves living through, living in, 'forms of life' that Wordsworth in his late twenties is looking back on. If literature is, in Henry James's phrase, only possible when one has achieved detachment, then so is the *study* of literature.

I offer the case of *The Prelude* not because it is distinctive but because it is, alas, representative. And it is representative in part because the influence of university departments of English and of the examinations syndicates is an excessively and improperly powerful one. A friend of mine, head of English in a comprehensive school, submitted a comprehensive and scrupulous critique of the Oxford 'A' level in Eng. lit. and proposals for an alternative curriculum. Receipt of his letter was acknowledged tersely, with a note to the effect that he would in due course be receiving a considered reply; that was eighteen months ago, and he has not yet received a reply. He was also one of a group of high school English teachers invited to Oxford to discuss the 'O' and 'A' level syllabuses with some of the Oxford dons involved in the setting of exams. He was, in his own words, treated like a naughty boy. So, people whose special competence is in post-doctoral *arcana* are deciding what fifteen-year-olds shall read! A bizarre illustration of the fact that the "major control on the structuring of knowledge at the secondary level is the structuring of knowledge at the tertiary level, specifically the university" (Basil Bernstein 'On the Classification and Framing of Educational Knowledge', in M. F. D. Young (ed), *Knowledge and Control*, Collier-Macmillan, 1971).

But let's return to the graduate student-teacher. When he embarks on his teaching practice, he is, for the first time in three years, participating – other than privately – in the world that lies outside the encapsulated university ghetto. He is, for the first time in over three years, accountable to people whose terms of appeal are other than those current in the university English department. And if he is perceptive, if he can afford to be so, if he has the resilience to allow himself to be so, he will very soon observe with a peculiar intimacy what James Agee observed:

'It would be hard to make clear enough . . . in what different worlds words and processes leave a teacher, and reach a child. Children, taught either years beneath their intelligence or miles wide of relevance to it, or both: their intelligence becomes hopelessly bewildered, drawn off its centres, bored, or atrophied. . . .'[1]

Perceiving such a dichotomy, or, more likely, perceiving the legacy of such a dichotomy – the strangely biddable, conscientious, comatose condition of aspiring sixth formers – the student-teacher has to make a decision. And we know that the making of decisions takes place at both rational and irrational levels: at moments of stress, we tend to panic, and to decide out of panic, out of our own ego-needs.

One decision is to press on authoritatively with the 'set book' and this is the decision that most of us have been making for the past seventy years.[2] And it is the decision that the student-teacher will make, if he has any professional aspirations. After all, he has recently 'got up' Wordsworth for finals and is not in a position cheerfully to recognise that, *vis-à-vis* the question of the-'meaning'-of-Wordsworth-to-seventeen-year-olds, he is in no sense an authority.

An alternative decision would be to adandon the set book and to plough an independent furrow, but such a decision, resting in a decent autonomy, is not of course available to most of us.[3] At root, the choice, to use Wörringer's terms, is between abstraction and empathy. The way of abstraction is to appeal to *a priori* or supervening, institutional or precedent, premises: the self is thus absolved. The way of empathy rests on a responsiveness to one's pupils, to who they are, and to where they are. Historically, our 'best pupils have replicated ourselves and maintained a tidy well-ordered universe; ideally, all of our pupils will become, variously, their best selves, continuing to delight in human variousness.

But the way of empathy is difficult, because it involves one in a complicated triangular relationship – the 'subject', one's pupils and one's self. And it involves a radical appraisal of what is found at each corner of the triangle. So, the questions multiply, hydra-headed. One such question is 'What is literature?' Now, oddly or evenly, this is a question that very few English graduates have ever been encouraged or asked to entertain. It is, of course, a very un-English kind of question and the reaction of many teachers of literature is to shrug the shoulders of indifference or to expel the snort of impatience. Since we have not been taught to attend to the question, we assume either that it doesn't exist or that, if it does, it is trivial, best left to the picky-picky toils of French existentialists or of Eastern European social anthropologists. But, in the event, for the teacher of literature it *is* an important question, even if we don't feel competent to answer it: it is a question that we must at least ask, if we are not merely to perpetuate an unexamined *status quo*. Significantly, such answers as we can draw on for help are to be found, not so much within the limits of literary criticism, as such, but rather in the writings of such diverse and ostensibly promiscuous figures as George Kelly, Wallace Stevens, Jean-Paul Sartre, Edward Thompson and Michael Oakeshott, all of whom provide us, in their several ways, with a language for speaking of the written word in relation to the lives of those who make it and of those who receive, or choose not to receive, it.[4]

I am pleading not for a sociology of literature, or a politics of literature, or a psychopathology of literature – useful and necessary as such pursuits are – to displace a criticism of literature; rather, for a view of literature which will see it, both historically and currently, as a special form of those utterances which characterise the daily lives of all human beings. The problem for the student-teacher is to come to know the fabric, the rhythms, the tensions, the idioms of the daily lives of his pupils in such a way that the literature that he shares with them, or makes available to them, will meet them, as it were, on their own ground. The problem is one of establishing connections, fructifying, generative, mind-enlivening, thought-provoking connections. (This is not, I need hardly add, to deny the literature of fantasy or of the exotic. If *Beowulf* is not 'about' the darkness *within ourselves*, then I have no idea what it could conceivably be about. Kids of eight, nine, or ten 'know' this, but it seems to escape philologically-disposed undergraduates.)

In such a way, we simply transcend or subvert the weary distinctions between mass-education and elitist education. The activities which go into making an important novel or a great poem are, in a useful sense, already there in the on-going conduct of our pupils. Useful, because if we point the attention of our pupils toward *their own* behaviour, they will perceive intimate, familiar and genial paradigms of the arts of fiction, drama and poetry.

But the 'dialect' of literature is, with a few bizarre exceptions, the standard dialect, I hear you cry. And most of our pupils are suffering not only from a non-standard dialect, but from one that is linguistically – lexically and syntactically – impoverished. The social and historical roots of the myth of 'impoverishment' or of 'deprivation' have not yet been adequately explored, but the myth has certainly been pervasive for at least a hundred years. One finds it embedded in the writings of otherwise decent, honourable and sensitive people such as Matthew Arnold and George Sampson, both of whom have had significant influences on the history of English teaching.

It derives some of its strength and survival value from the un-examined and persuasive analogy of physical or economic deprivation; it occurs most emphatically in the writings of men whose main, or only, contact with the 'lower orders' has been through institutional, formal and hierarchically disposed channels; and it reinforces the implicit assumption of those who embody the fruits of mainstream middle-class culture, that they 'possess', enjoy and benefit from certain linguistic privileges which, in all fairness, they should make available to the less fortunate. A decent enough notion, to be sure, but wrong-headed.

The cards, therefore, are continuously stacked against the non-standard dialect: the standard and non-standard meet on the standard's own ground. The standard has the professional status and prestige – the power lies with the standard: it holds the keys. So our teaching of English for the last hundred years has been based on the unexamined premise that the standard dialect is the *unum necessarium* and, even when the matter has been researched, it has been approached and slanted from the viewpoint and value-system of the standard.[5]

I suppose I am fortunate in having grown up as a speaker of a refractory and distinctive non-standard dialect – that of the Black Country – and I am fortunate now in living in a Yorkshire village, where I can enjoy unaffected and disinterested friendship with speakers of another non-standard dialect. And when I see my village friends lapsing into a relative inarticulacy in the presence of an assertively condescending speaker of the standard, I can recall my own 'strategies of silence' during my years in grammar school and university.

The relative longevity of the myth of deprivation – the cant of 'the disadvantaged', which muddles educational liberalism both here and in the States – and the unexamined high status of the myth: these are testimony to the fact that higher education in the humanities has its own distinctive prestige dialect, plays its own peculiar symbolic games. And so is the corollary that possession of the dialect is a necessary entrance qualification to the great company of the sheep, the elect, the arrived.

The social and educational ramifications of the dialect-problem are many and various. I recall the years that I spent teaching in comprehensive schools in the Midlands, schools where most of the kids spoke my own native dialect. Many of my colleagues proceeded on the assumption that their pupils' speech was 'lazy', but they themselves made no effort to learn the dialect of their pupils. The teachers were encapsulated in small pockets of suburban standard, and failed continuously to detect the expressive and fine nuances of the local dialect. I recall an otherwise honourable headmaster, who complained to me that he found many of the kids' parents to be rude in their social address. I had to reply that, on the contrary, they were being *polite*, but that he didn't understand the dialect of their politeness.

One could instance thousands of such misapprehensions, but I want to turn to another feature of the situation: nowhere are social and dialectal assumptions more firmly embedded than in the way we have conceived of the English literature curriculum. In this matter, the dominant paradigm has been a colonial or missionary one: we, the teachers, bring culture to the benighted savages of the inner city. For a variety of reasons, good and bad, the 'bright' pupils join forces with the missionaries and go off to higher education so that, eventually transformed into bible-bearers, they can return and themselves bring the light of the word into the places of darkness. The pupils who don't see the point are consigned to the status of 'also rans'.

The persisting model of giver, gift, and receiver; of enlightening or of civilising; of entry to the elitist citadel; the model, in a word, of The Word, will not do, except for the purposes of the Black

F

Paper Jeremiahs. We need to follow a lead offered by Kenneth Keniston:

'The advocate, reformer, or myth maker faces an almost super-human task: he must first of all unearth the very values that he will then attempt to develop, illustrate, enhance, and implement. . . .
'Language is a prerequisite of cure. One way of looking at in-dividual psychotherapy is to view it as a means of acquiring an adequate language (in the broadest sense of the word) for hitherto unexpressed feelings and impulses.'[6]

The 'very values' that the teacher of English can help his pupils to develop, that he can illustrate, enhance, and implement – these very values are available to him in the current, on-going, available 'forms of life',[7] available in the sense that, if the teacher allows and encourages his pupils to offer them to others in the classroom – stories, jokes, anecdotes, puzzlements, questions, surmises, specula-tions, wonderings, amazements, attractions and revulsions, delights, discoveries and so on – they form a nexus of representations of living which are *also* offered, in turn, by literature.

Further, we must add to this a notion which is expressed with convenient brevity by Liam Hudson: 'the psychologist should en-visage his work as a process wherein *one person becomes acquainted with others*'[8] (Hudson's italics).

I suggest that, at present, the urgent function of the teacher is to set up situations, in his classroom, whereby kids may the more readily 'acquire an adequate language' by *never* being given to under-stand that their current language is *in any sense* inadequate. And that the classroom 'society' in which this takes place should be one in which 'one person becomes acquainted with others'. But I must add a further paradox, that the pupils themselves should not be *explicitly* invited to conceive of their English lessons in terms of 'becoming acquainted with others'. The act of 'becoming acquainted' should be experienced, entered into, shared, and enjoyed, but it must never be the naked goal or aim of the pupils. If it is, we enter the cul-de-sac of self-consciousness. A brief example will serve to illustrate my point: the teacher reads, to a class of twelve-year-olds, John Crow Ransom's poem, 'Janet Waking', a poem about a girl whose pet hen suddenly dies and who is plunged into uncompre-hending grief. The poem's reading is repeated and then there is a brief silence. Not a silence in which the kids wait to be interrogated, but a silence in which the poem is 'taken in' and in which recognitions occur. Then a pupil breaks the silence: "That's like what happened to. . . ." For the rest of the lesson the kids speak about similar experiences in their own past lives and so become 'acquainted with others'; they are unwittingly naming the hitherto unnameable and, in so doing, they are 'acquiring an adequate language'.

Linguists have provided us with a useful distinction, between 'competence' and 'performance': many 'competences' remain 'unperformed' in the absence of propitious or supportive contexts. My argument is this: that our first responsibility as teachers of English is to allow, encourage, promote, invite 'performance'. But this is not to be confused with 'verbal display', the kind of linguistic exhibition, of juggling with fashionable jargon, which American students describe as a 'snow job', in which they make the kinds of sounds which teachers reward them for making. An example from an American graduate student: 'The Existential Anti-Hero in the Novels of Camus and Sartre'. An essay with that kind of title is simply an occasion for a highly conventionalised, almost ritualistic, display of the requisite tokens. One of my most intelligent students at York tells me that it was in this way that he gained a distinction in 'S' level English.

All kids, it seems to me, can speak coherently, with power and purpose, if *we* can refrain from preventing them. But if we continue to insist on measuring them in terms of their capacity to ape our own dialect, our own well-worn ways of degutting *The Prelude*, then we are, willy-nilly, forced to separate them into sheep and goats, into those who are willing or able to provide teacher-rewarding behaviour, and those who are not.

'Hitherto unexpressed feelings and impulses': there are various 'locations' for the expression of such feelings and impulses: the autobiography, the anecdote, the fiction, the tall story, the poem, the improvisation. Nowhere is the discovery of the possibility of such expression more startling and more satisfying than in the field of dramatic improvisation, but it is difficult to write about it. It's significant that one of our best teachers of improvisation, Dorothy Heathcote, has not been persuaded to write a book. It is virtually impossible to give a full account of her ways of interacting with pupils, even within the confines of an hour. But, for our purposes, certain features are significant.

'For its expression, dramatic improvisation demands crystallisation of ideas *in groups*. . . . It can employ the individuals, *working as a group*, to conceive the ideas, area, and level of interest in the first place. . . . It draws directly upon the individual's life and subjective experiences as its basic material. . . . Dramatic activity is concerned with the crises, the turning points of life, large and small, which cause people to reflect and take note. . . . It allows children to employ their own views of life and people, use their own standards of evaluation, and exercise their own terms when expressing and tempering these ideas.'[9]

Such a conception of an *educative* activity is, of course, very different indeed from the traditional, academic notion that drama is reading a Shakespeare play in the sixth form, taking care to ensure that the pupils have a dictionary definition of every word in the text. It is centrally different in that it both uses and respects the pupil's own experience, allows them to use their own un-redeemed language, and attend to the questions – political, social, personal – that occupy *their* minds. And it's no accident that some of Dorothy's most exciting work has been done with delinquent adolescents and with the inmates of a mental hospital. In such work, her 'students' move towards 'an adequate language' and 'become acquainted with others'.

The role of the teacher in such work is, of course, far from that of bringer of The Word or mediator of the prestige culture. In Dorothy Heathcote's words:

'The teacher's role is often seen as a consistent one – that of "he who knows and can therefore tell or instruct". This is too limited a register, and a barren one to boot, except in certain circumstances. In drama the teacher must be prepared to fulfil many roles:

The deliberate opposer of the common view in order to give feedback and aid clarity of thought.
The narrator who helps to set mood and register of events.
The positive withdrawer who "lets them get on with it".
The suggester of ideas, as a group member.
The supporter of tentative leadership.
The "dogsbody" who discovers material and drama aids.
The reflector who is used by the children to assess their statements.
The arbiter in argument.
The deliberately obtuse one, who requires to be informed and the one who "*believes that the children can do it*".'[10]

What kinds of resources does the teacher need to possess, before he can adequately fulfil these roles? Will they be promoted, supplied, extended, refined by a training in literary criticism as currently practised? I simply pose the unanswerable questions. One thing, however, is clear: that the teacher needs to acquire the capacity to engage in a great variety of social interactions, to think, feel, and respond on his feet, and to resist being trapped within a limited and stereotypic set of roles – the asker of factual questions, the interrogator and so on. In this respect, I suspect that three years spent in reading Eng. lit. is actually injurious.[11]

If the teacher of English is to find adequate models for his own professional 'style', he must look not only to outstanding and exemplary mavericks such as Dorothy Heathcote, but also to the ways in which others, in non-academic fields, acquire competence or, indeed, mastery. How, for example, does one 'become' an artist, armed with appropriately resourceful technical skills? The question may seem irrelevant, even frivolous, yet the answers that the American sculptor, Frank Gallo, has given to this question are extremely apropos. The whole of Gallo's statement is worth looking up,[12] but I quote him as he attends to one or two crucial issues:

Holden: Were you always a figurative artist, or did you go through a phase when you were abstract?
Gallo: When I was an undergraduate in the fifties, everybody was teaching abstract art. However, abstract art was a *painting* technique, so as a sculptor I didn't get too much pressure to work abstractly. We did have to take painting courses, but I was never satisfied to paint in the abstract. What are you learning? You're learning how to make a better abstract painting, but you're not growing.
Holden: Were you considered square for not doing abstract sculpture?
Gallo: I wasn't with it too much. Abstract art lends itself to teaching so easily: you teach rhythm and composition, and you never have any emotional content at all, no personality interference. It's the ideal subject for teaching.
Holden: How did you learn about the figure? How did you learn about anatomy, about how to put the right pieces in the right places?
Gallo: What makes you think you *need* to learn certain things? Every kid knows how to draw. Every kid knows how to sing.

No one told me I didn't know anything about the figure. I assumed I *did* know, because I was interested in the figure. I think that my things were anatomically correct from the very beginning. I don't think anatomy is so hard to learn, being a body yourself. I don't think you need to be trained to do some things that I feel are natural to some people. When you look at the art of primitive cultures, you can't say who taught these people. They could all sing, chant, pray, work magic, sculpt, make beautiful arrowheads, and make all kinds of beautiful things. I don't like the idea that you have to be trained to make something beautiful. The thought that anyone needs to be *trained* to know about human anatomy seems peculiar. I learned a lot from girls; maybe I haven't got a photographic memory, but I have a good tactile memory.

Holden: But you say you learned a lot from Ernie Moll. What did he teach you?

Gallo: I don't remember what he taught me. I think you learn by hanging around with artists. You become friends with people of similar inclinations and interests. If you hang around with artists, you've got to learn something.

If, then, we are to get into a fruitful, generative, useful relationship with our 'non-academic'[13] pupils, to be of use to them, I think we have to think of our role as essentially collaborative: we are engaged in the same pursuit as they are. But, in order to do so, we have to stop thinking of ourselves as people who wrote some rather clever, rather successful literary critical essays as undergraduates. We have to learn to think of ourselves as people, like our pupils, engaged in moving towards a fuller and more adequate articulacy in representing those matters that really do matter to us, in celebrating those aspects of our lives that call for celebration, in exploring the subtler, more elusive, more mysteriously problematical aspects of our lives. It is a tall order, but nothing else will really do.

Above all, we must abandon our *de haut en bas* postures: we didn't always have them. We learned them, at school and university; and we can unlearn them, in relating, collaboratively and mutually, with our pupils. In so doing, we shall discover that the need is to change or repair not the kids but the institutions; to make them more immediately responsive to legitimate human needs and aspirations; to make them into places where kids are not taught to be ashamed of the way in which they and their parents speak, and where teachers do not continuously insult and destroy the living language of their pupils. If you destroy my language, you destroy my world, and it's no excuse to claim that your intentions were honourable.

Historically, we have taught children to distrust their language and, *pari passu*, to distrust their experience. Our high schools have said to the twelve-year-child: we are not interested in your lives – you know nothing – and you have no adequate language. The result has been, for many of us, a state of anomie: we really don't know who we are. And we have gone through university and entered the teaching profession, alienated from our selves, and from our own past.[14]

The result is that we force our pupils to do those things that they are 'no good at', those things which fail to engage their minds and hearts; and we prevent them from extending their strengths, those activities and forms which exemplify their sense of power and purpose.

My university colleagues spend much of their time talking and writing of phenomena of which they have no *immediate* experience; my village neighbours speak only of those things which they have personally apprehended. The former is our model of the educated mind; the latter is our image of the deprived!

It must be clear that, accepting such a view of the relationship between the study of English and the teaching of the subject, potential teachers of English cannot help but benefit from community service experience at every stage in their own development, whether as pupils in sixth forms, students at university, or as student-teachers. Such activity, within specific situations demanding effective collaborative action, will clearly provide the learner-teacher with significant experience, both linguistically and culturally. It may, particularly, move his consciousness in such directions that he will feel impatient with literary studies as currently practised: it may indeed point him towards recognising the usefulness of socio-linguistics. In any event, I can only hope that the English departments of our universities will respond positively and generously to the provocations that such a student can, and very likely will, offer them.

REFERENCES

1   James Agee, *Let Us Now Praise Famous Men*, Ballantine Books, New York, 1970, p 282.
2   See David Shayer, *The Teaching of English in Schools, 1900–1970*, Routledge & Kegan Paul, 1972, *passim.*
3   An extraordinary case of cheerful and productive free enterprise is provided by Eliot Wigginton. The fruits – or some of them – of his work are available in the magazine *Foxfire*, a magazine written and illustrated by his pupils. A selection from the magazines is available in *The Foxfire Book*, Doubleday, New York, 1972. Its message is fairly close to that of *Letter to A Teacher from the School of Barbiana*: it has to do with allowing pupils to find and/or preserve a sense of worth. The subtitle of *The Foxfire Book* is: 'Hog dressing, log cabin building, mountain crafts and foods, planting by the signs, snake lore, hunting tales, faith healing, moonshining, and other affairs of plain living.'
4   See, for example, E. P. Thompson, *Education and Experience*, Leeds University Press.
5   See William Labov, 'The Logic of Nonstandard English', in P. P. Giglioli (ed) *Language and Social Context*, Penguin Books, 1972.
6   'The Decline of Utopia', in *Youth and Dissent*, Harcourt Brace Jovanovich, New York, 1971, pp 52–3.
7   The phrase is from Wittgenstein. See George Pitcher (ed), *Wittgenstein: The Philosophical Investigations*, Doubleday, New York, 1966, *passim.*
8   Liam Hudson, *The Cult of Fact*, Jonathan Cape, 1972, p. 162.
9   From 'Drama', an address given to the 1969 annual conference of NATE, published in *English in Education*, vol 3, no. 2, Summer 1969, published by NATE in association with OUP.
10   Ibid., pp 62–3.
11   'Injurious' may seem a strong word, and indeed it is so. But think of the way in which one of the mainstreams of undergraduate activity is inescapably, and too often reductively, analytical. Then consider the many other uses of the mind that kids' lives actually contain.
12   In *The American Artist*, March, 1972.
13   On this libellous term, cf. Ian Crichton Smith:
    'You cannot say "Not-Adam." You cannot say "Not-Eve."
    The apple has a name as well. . . .'
    From 'Shall Gaelic Die?' in *Selected Poems*, Gollancz, 1970.
14   A more measured way of putting this is offered by Nell Keddie: 'It would appear that the willingness to take over the teacher's definition of what is to constitute the problem and what is to count as knowledge may require pupils to regard as irrelevant or inappropriate what they might see as problems in a context of everyday meaning' ('Classroom Knowledge', in Michael F. D. Young (ed) *Knowledge and Control*, Collier-Macmillan, 1971, p. 151).

Chapter Four

Law Students and Community Action

BY MICHAEL ZANDER

Michael Zander is Reader in Law at the London School of Economics, London University. He was educated at Cambridge and Harvard. He practised as a solicitor in a City firm and then joined LSE in 1963 and *The Guardian* in the same year, as its Legal Correspondent. He has written extensively on problems of the profession, legal services especially to the poor, and administration of justice and the criminal process. Among his writings are *Lawyers and the Public Interest*, 1968, *Unequal Rights* (with R. M. Titmuss), 1968, and *What's Wrong with the Law?* (editor), 1970.

If the law is anything, it is a practical discipline which derives virtually its entire meaning from the solving of real-life problems. Yet the subject is taught in the class-room as if the real world barely existed. The law student devotes almost the whole of his time to the decisions of the higher courts and to the writings of textbook authors. Problems are presented in tidy parcels, neatly compartmentalised into tort, crime, contract, etc. He never sees the messiness of real-life situations. It is not merely that he never glimpses a client. He normally does not even gain training in advocacy or bargaining or negotiating or interviewing. His education is bookish and abstract. It focuses on theories, rules and concepts – rarely on the underlying context of the economic, social and political facts.

Most law students work fairly hard but it would probably be true to say that few are much excited by what they are doing. The atmosphere of most law faculties is worthy but dull. From the start to the end of their courses they tend to repeat over and over again the same routine – the lecture, the weekly or fortnightly essays written in haste by paraphrasing the text-book or analysing a few cases, and the four or five three-hour examination papers in each of the three years, demanding five answers out of ten questions.

Law faculties have been extraordinarily conservative and un-adventurous in developing new methods of teaching or examining. Only a few, for instance, have yet experimented with the 6,000 to 8,000 word essay as a means of stretching the student intellectually beyond the fairly pitiful demands of the weekly tutorial essay. Equally, virtually none have yet thought of how to get the student out of the library and into the community.

It would seem fairly obvious that exposure to real-life situations might make a contribution to legal education. On the simplest level, it would teach the student, through personal observation, something about how the law operates in practice. Frequently, it would reveal the critical difference between what is written in the books and what actually occurs. More often, it might teach him things that are never dealt with in the books at all.

For several years now, I have tried to expose students to at least a smattering of knowledge of one or another aspect of the legal system. At the end of each first year, in the period immediately after the examinations, when most students are doing little before going down for the vacation, I have put on some form of practical exercise on a voluntary–compulsory basis. Generally most students do participate. It started originally as a courts visiting programme, but soon expanded into an annual study of some actual problem. We looked at the way in which courts handled bail applications, at the kinds of cases in which defendants in the criminal courts were unrepresented, and at tenants' knowledge of the rent acts and of the possibility of getting their rents reduced. We investigated whether retail shops complied with the regulations for advertisements of credit terms. We asked in police stations about the information available to suspects about their legal rights.

All the studies produced publishable results – and all in areas where there was either no knowledge, or very little. The students appear to have enjoyed participating in the projects and, at the same time, by dint of their considerable manpower, were able, in the short period of a week, to get statistically worthwhile results. (It is vital, of course, that the person conducting such enterprises should have the necessary basic minimum of knowledge of the methodology of social research to ensure the validity of the results. It is grossly wasteful of the students' time if they are put to work on a project the results of which cannot be used because of some defect in the planning.)

To judge at least from published studies, few other law teachers have yet appreciated the very evident value of putting student numbers to good use in assaying how the legal system operates. (One exception is Mr Stephen White of Southampton University, who has published studies based on observation of the use of probation reports in the lower courts, and of judicial homilies in sentencing.) But published results are far from being the only test of quality or use and several teachers have sent their students to observe different aspects of the operation of the legal system. If each student looks at some different problem it may be rare for his report to justify publication – simply because law students, even working under supervision, may lack the ability or the means to mount a sufficiently comprehensive inquiry. But several students working together may, through team work and the extra hours, to some extent make good their collective inexperience.

There is little knowledge yet as to whether law students can be used effectively to interview respondents on a formal questionnaire, but it would certainly seem worth attempting, as this would open an important methodological tool of inquiry. A measure of interviewer training would be necessary and assistance from the sociology or social administration department may be invaluable to ensure that the questionnaire, the research design and sample drawing are adequate to the task in hand.

But all these types of operations suffer from being basically passive – the student is not himself working in the situation: he is merely observing, measuring, recording or describing what he sees or hears. Many students would derive even greater benefit from actually making use of such legal skills as they may already have developed.

My own first attempt to get something of this kind going was in the form of a legal advice facility, manned by law students of the London School of Economics, for fellow-students at LSE and the technical, secretarial and administrative staff. The service has functioned in term-time since autumn 1970, on Monday and Friday, between 1 p.m. and 2 p.m. Usually there are about six or seven student advisers who process the clients – with the help, if needed, of the faculty member, who is required always to be present.

The participants first thought that other students would be reluctant to bring their problems to a student-run advice service. But this lack of self-confidence has been wholly confounded by what has happened. Almost from the outset, the advice service has dealt with a large number of problems covering a wide range of matters. Many, naturally, have concerned landlord-tenant problems, but a surprising proportion relate to quite different matters – divorce, consumer problems, missing charter flights, holiday pay disputes, even suits against university authorities. If the matter can be disposed of by oral or written advice, the students will normally handle the case – subject always to faculty supervision and guidance. If letters have to be written, the faculty member will approve and sign them – though the first draft will be prepared by the student involved. If a solicitor in private practice is required, for instance to issue a writ, the client is assisted to find a suitable firm.

The service has already performed a doubly valuable function – of giving the student participants some experience of real problems and, at the same time, of providing a practical and useful outlet for their energies.

The next stage is to see whether the service, which has so far been confined to the School itself, can be expanded to take in some form of community action. The best possibility seems to be some form of facility designed to provide representation in tribunals for ordinary people, who lack the means to employ a lawyer and have no one else who can appear for them. There is no legal aid for cases heard by tribunals and yet many of the problems are both complex and important in their economic consequences. (A wrong decision, depriving a claimant of the whole or part of his entitlement to welfare benefits, may sound a minor matter when expressed in weekly terms, but over a period of years the amount at stake is often very substantial.) Few applicants in rent tribunals, supplementary benefit tribunals, national insurance tribunals and the like are represented and, although law students may not be the equal of qualified lawyers, they may be a considerable improvement on nothing at all, especially if they first receive a measure of training.

Although there are several universities or polytechnics where this kind of service is under consideration, there are as yet few where it is operational. There is, however, already a very great deal of experience with this kind of enterprise in the United States where, over the past three to four years, there has been a veritable explosion of action-based academic programmes. It seems entirely probable that, with the advantage of hindsight, it will be seen in fifty years time that this development marks the single most important step forward in legal education of the present century. Certainly, it has already begun to transform the style and manner of American legal education – which even before this was, in so many ways, superior to any available in Britain. No less than 125 of the 147 accredited American law schools have, in the past few years, established practical training (known as clinical) programmes in which students, supervised by faculty members, work in a variety of real-life situations.

So far, this extremely significant movement has attracted little attention in this country. Yet there is no question that it could be adapted for use here.

The forms of clinical programmes vary greatly, both from one university to another and within the same law school. One common model is a legal advice facility in a prison manned by students under faculty supervision. There are now over fifty law schools which provide such a service.

Usually, it consists of assistance in preparing petitions for post-conviction relief (American procedure permits many more diverse forms of challenge to a conviction than our own). The students interview clients in the prison and then work on the problem at the law school. Many programmes also handle prisoners' civil problems. Some offer representation to inmates charged with disciplinary offences in the prison, or for parole eligibility. Some are even allowed to assist prisoners wishing to take legal proceedings against the prison authorities.

In some programmes, the students handle any case that comes their way. In others, the supervising faculty member takes only those which appear to offer educational value. Each student usually has his own case-load.

At Yale, for example, there is a programme at the Danbury Federal Penitentiary. Twenty law students work with two practising attorneys. Inmates state the nature of the problem on application forms. Students then do preliminary research, conduct interviews at the prison, undertake whatever further research is needed and, if the case has merit, draft appropriate letters or pleadings. At each stage, faculty attorneys supervise and advise the students. No legal advice is given, or action taken, without prior approval of the supervisors.

A training and orientation course prepares the students to handle cases. Each beginner is given basic instruction from older student supervisors and by the supervising attorneys. His first visits to the prison are as an observer.

Inmates with access to lawyers in private practice naturally use them, but the service offered by students is accepted gratefully by many who would otherwise have no one to assist them. The quality of work is generally high – often higher than that of busy practitioners.

Fears on the part of prison authorities, that student involvement in prison would promote trouble, have not been realised. On the contrary, students, by showing interest in prisoners' problems, have often managed to defuse complaints and reduce bitterness.

Another typical model of clinical practice is the running or participation in the work of a neighbouring law firm. At Harvard, for instance, the students man a fully-fledged neighbourhood law firm in a poor area in Cambridge, Massachusetts. The office is run by some five supervising attorneys who utilise the part-time services of some 100 or more students. Each student has an interviewing period of some one and a half hours per week. These hours are staggered so that there are always at least two students on duty at any one time. The student is fully responsible for his case-load, although he works under the supervision of one of the qualified lawyers. Before commencing work in the office, the new intake of students are given an intensive four day training course in the most typical kinds of problems they may meet in practice. Cases, and issues arising from them, are discussed both with the supervising attorney and in seminars.

The office provides not only ordinary service work for clients, but a variety of preventive and law reform functions. The students conduct courses in law in the Cambridge high schools. They prepare and distribute a series of community education booklets, explaining legal rights and responsibilities of, for instance, welfare recipients, tenants, public utility users and consumers. They have drafted legislation for enactment by the State legislature and have not only lobbyed legislators but have prepared client groups to testify at legislative hearings. Several bills originated by the students have been passed into law. The office has also been involved in a number of test cases in the courts.

Hoftsra Law School in Nassua County, New York has a neighbourhood firm run by faculty members with the help of students. About twenty students, almost a third of the second-year class, take part in the work of the office. Each student is expected to spend at least seven hours a week on office work, though many spend considerably more. The office accepts only cases that appear to offer educational value.

At first students only sit in on interviews, but gradually, as they master the technique, they are permitted to conduct their own interviews. They write first drafts of all legal papers and do research of legal problems. All work is supervised by the qualified attorneys. In many law schools the programme consists primarily of representation of indigent persons in court. One programme of this kind ˙at the University of Denver has actually been functioning for sixty-five years. Colorado was one of the first states to grant students in an accredited law school a right of audience, subject to supervision by qualified lawyers. (Thirty-eight states have by now given students a right of audience under supervision of academic or other qualified lawyers.) The clerk of the Denver county court notifies the student office that counsel has been requested for a particular case. The student sees the client at his home or, if he is being held in custody, in jail. Student counsel handle the case from start to finish – though supervising attorneys are available to assist whenever necessary. Most students handle two or three cases per quarter.

In the neighbouring Jefferson County Court, students act as duty counsel for indigent defendants, advising on pleas. In the Legal Aid Society Internship Programme, students handle a variety of civil and juvenile cases. They represent clients in small tort cases, debt collections, landlord-tenant disputes and wage claims. The domestic relations court students process divorce cases.

Some programmes place students with the local prosecutor's office, or with the Public Defender. At Boston University, for example, there has been a Public Defender project since 1964. Thirty third-year students take part, under the supervision of an experienced practitioner, who is employed as Clinical Professor. Cases assigned by the judge as indigent, which do not go to the state's Public Defender office, are allocated to the student service. In a period from January to June, the programme may act as counsel for as many as 800 defendants.

On the basis of the success of this operation, Boston Law School has, since 1967, operated a Prosecutor Programme supervised by an experienced District Attorney. Thirty third-year students take part, divided into ten teams of three students each. Cases are assigned to the team and the students take turns in trying the assigned case whilst the other two assist in the preparation for trial, interviewing witnesses and in research.

A similar double programme exists at Harvard. The Defender Office was founded in 1949 to assist indigent defendants. The staff consists of 35 first-year, 35 second-year and 15 third-year students, selected on the basis of interest, experience in criminal law and interview. Only third-year students may appear in court, but the others do preparatory work, including interviews with clients. The Harvard Student District Attorney's office dates from 1966. Third-year students participating handle cases on their own, under the direction of a District Attorney, who is specially assigned to this work. The students also handle the prosecution on appeal in cases where the defendant opts for the speedy six man jury, instead of trial by a full jury of twelve.

At New York University, a student can opt for one or more of eleven different clinical courses. Students in the consumer credit course are attached to the New York City Department of Consumer Affairs, where they engage in research on specific legal problems and assist in the preparation and conduct of administrative proceedings. Some of the students doing the Juvenile Delinquency course are assigned to the office of the Corporation Counsel, where they conduct cases for the prosecution, or to the Legal Aid office, where they assist defence counsel. Two are attached to the New York Legislative Committee on Child Abuse, where they undertake research and statutory drafting.

Some eighteen NYU students work under direction in a Labour Law clinical programme, for one and a half days per week. In co-operation with the Mayor's Committee on Exploitation of Workers, they represent employees before the Unemployment Compensation Board, the Commission on Human Rights and in union disciplinary hearings. A law and psychiatry course has fifteen students who prepare case histories of patients in the prison ward, children's section or adolescent section of a New York mental hospital. Each student works on his case with a co-operating psychiatrist. He attends medical conferences, psychiatric interviews and court certification hearings.

An Environmental Law Clinic allows six students to work with a public interest law firm specialising in environmental matters and with the Environmental Unit of the US Attorney's Office for the Southern District of New York. These courses are in addition to others at NYU which permit work in a neighbourhood law firm, and representation of indigent defendants in both civil and criminal law.

At Yale, in addition to the prison advice facility, there are courses enabling students to work in neighbourhood firms, in prosecutor offices and as public defenders. One course concentrates specifically on pre-trial detention. Students help pre-trial prisoners with a host of legal and social problems. Work in this seminar has produced research papers on such topics as Police Decisions to Release on Bail; the View from the Lock-Up; Delays and Pre-trial Detention on the Sixth Circuit; Work Release as a Pre-trial Alternative; and Classification in a Pre-trial Detention Institution.

Two Yale projects in mental hospitals permit students to help patients with problems of commitment, social security, ex-servicemen's pension rights, child custody and divorce.

Another approach at Yale is to allow students to undertake individual projects, under supervision of a faculty member or of a qualified lawyer outside the law school. For varying amounts of credit, a student can work on a case or problem of particular interest. In rare cases, students can even be given permission to work full-time for a whole semester on such a project. In one instance, for example, a student worked for a term with a non-profit public interest law firm. The work entailed research and design of a novel law reform action, challenging rules and practices in Washington, restricting the placement of the homeless and institutionalised children with families for foster-care and adoption. This involved discovering actual cases (through an advertisement in the local press) and gathering data on the child care institutions in the area.

The work of American law students in this great range of activities has drawn considerable favourable response from the Bar, Bench and the Administration. In the recent Supreme Court case which extended the right of counsel to misdemeanour cases involving jail sentences, Mr Justice Brennan's opinion mentioned law students as one source of legal counsel. 'Given the huge increase in law school enrolments over the past few years, I think it plain that law students can be looked to to make a significant contribution, quantitatively and qualitatively to the representation of the poor in many areas including cases reached by today's decision.' *Argersinger* v. *Hamlin*, 32 L, second edition, 530, 1972.

Chief Justice Burger himself has strongly encouraged the trend. Speaking at the American Bar Association's meeting in 1969 the Chief Justice criticised the traditional system of legal education based primarily on rules of law formulated by appeal courts. 'Does it not seem to you that the appellate case method of teaching may have really been a form of escapism from the depressing atmosphere

G

which surrounds the short and simple annals of the poor.' He welcomed the trend to permit students to become involved in the problems of the local community. This, he thought, was 'among the most encouraging developments in the past thirty years or more, but it represents hardly more than a slice of the available loaf of practical work which could be exploited in legal education'.

It is widely agreed among those experienced in this field that the quality of the work done and the educational value of the experience depend primarily on the extent and nature of the supervision. Many law schools have found that it is not educationally sound simply to send students to work in placements, say, with prosecutors, defenders, or government officers. In most cases, the scheme demands the employment by the law school of supervisors, who can take responsibility for the work done by the students. Opportunities for seminars and discussion of problems raised contributes greatly to the value of the course. Often the clinical course involves the writing of research papers based on a concrete problem that arose in practice. But evaluation of the work by the student himself, through discussion with fellow participants and with experienced practitioners, seems an essential ingredient of success.

The hiring of full-time or part-time practitioners makes the exercise relatively costly. Moreover a programme that operates outside the law faculty involves expenditure on such items as travel, telephone, secretarial help, stationery, postage and even court fees. If the project operates throughout the year, it normally has to use paid student help during the vacations. So far, the cost has been borne mainly by the Council for Legal Education in Professional Responsibility (CLEPR), which was established in September 1968 by the Ford Foundation with an initial grant of $5 million. A second slightly larger grant in 1972 has ensured the continuation of the funding for the next several years. After four years, CLEPR had made ninety-three grants, totalling $3·75 million.

The aim and purpose of CLEPR is to help law schools start clinical courses with a view to their taking them over at their own expense at the end of the experimental periods. It seems that this hope is likely to be realised as law schools all over the United States are accepting that the programme is sufficiently valuable to be continued, even when the expense must be borne by the institution, out of its ordinary budget.

The educational benefit to the students is considerable. At first, there is massive evidence that students who choose these programmes greatly enjoy them. They are stimulated and motivated to work immensely hard, frequently at a stage when they have become bored and dissatisfied with the ordinary law school courses. Secondly, the intellectual challenge of the untidy, real-life situation is often greater than when the problem is wrapped in the neat and artificial categories served up by law teachers. The involvement with live clients and real human problems is, for most students, vastly more interesting than yet more exercises with John Doe and Richard Roe in the classroom. Also, the experience of seeing the law in action is often an educationally valuable corrective to class work. It is instructive for students to focus on and then be able to discuss and evaluate the divergence between practice and theory.

The clinical experience may also help students to cope with their own problems of maturing into lawyers. In particular, the students have to learn the discipline of helping clients without becoming ensnared by too emotional an involvement in their problems. Through discussion of the clinical experience and their reaction to it with their teachers, they learn more about themselves than is usual in ordinary university courses. Finally, it is obvious that clinical education may have important benefits to the community served. Though this is not the main object of the exercise it is nevertheless by no means a trivial or unimportant consequence.

For all these benefits to accrue, it is vital that the teachers who run the programmes take the trouble to sift the case-load so as to produce as many educationally interesting problems as possible in the available time. The purpose of the programme should not be to provide another service agency handling the full range of ordinary run of the mill problems. There will be time enough for this if and when the student eventually becomes a practitioner. Nor should the programme be 'good works' – the student may or may not choose to devote himself to charitable enterprises in his spare time, but the justification of clinical programmes should be that they are educationally sound and valuable. The purpose of the clinical programme must be to use real-life situation as a vehicle for clearer insights into the nature of law and its functions.

Could such a development occur in this country? The students are, admittedly, younger and less highly motivated in a professional sense. A higher proportion do not intend to become practitioners than is true in the US. Also, there is, as yet, no organisation or foundation that could be relied on for finance. There are obvious problems in finding supervising lawyers with sufficient practical experience and teaching ability. There are difficulties in formulating methods of examination for field work – though these have been surmounted in many other disciplines. If, as is probably the case, the ordinary methods of examination make little sense in this context, there is the problem of persuading faculties that credit should be given for work done without any examination at all. Certainly, unless credit can be given toward the degree, clinical legal education will never prosper. But this is not to say that the whole bait need be swallowed at the first bite.

If clinical legal education is to get under way in this country, it is probable that the first steps must be through voluntary, unpaid work done for the experience rather than for credit. My own experience at the London School of Economics shows that large numbers of students can quite easily be persuaded to give up their time to take part in studies of the legal process. LSE law students have also shown that, with supervision, they can run a part-time legal advice service for the benefit of fellow students and other members of the University. Similar enterprises have started at other institutions. There seems every reason to suppose that students would respond at least as well if given the opportunity to undertake more challenging tasks. Undoubtedly there are difficulties, but they need not be insuperable. All that is required is for two or three law faculties to show the way. The doubters would quickly be persuaded if they could see the idea working in practice.

Chapter Five

Community Service and Community Planning - Whose Ideals?

BY JUDITH ALLEN AND JOHN PALMER

Judith Allen is a lecturer in the Department of Social and Environmental Planning at the Polytechnic of Central London. She was educated in the United States of America where she studied Economics and Regional Planning. She is primarily concerned with relating curriculum development and innovative teaching techniques to the methodological problems of research in planning.

John A. D. Palmer is senior lecturer in Planning at the Polytechnic of Central London. After experience in local government planning departments in London and the South East, he joined a small group of activists forming the Notting Hill Housing Service, which worked in close association with a number of community groups, and in developing approaches to bringing together resources and expertise for community organisations to use, in developing their own programmes. He is currently attempting to link these problems with the education of town planners.

INTRODUCTION

The ideal of public service is one of the most important elements in the ethics of professionalism. Yet this ideal is open to interpretation in widely varying ways, and the particular interpretation adopted by a profession depends on many factors.[1] In this paper we examine the way Town Planners have interpreted this ideal, and argue that it has led to conservatism in the practice of town planning, and in the education of planners. A new interpretation of the ideal of public service is needed, one which takes into account the political aspects of planning. We argue that such a reformulation of the ideal will result in a new style of planning – which is coming to be known as Community Planning – and in the main body of the paper we turn our attention to the kind of education, formal and field-based, needed to develop a co-operative approach to the public service ideal in planning.

The convergence of these ideals, the attitudes which supported them,[2] and the needs of an emerging profession led to a number of latent problems which were highlighted by the programme of the post-1945 welfare state. Most of the important elements in the re-appraisal of town planning stem from this period, which was at the same time the high point of the profession's activities to date. Firstly, with the coming into operation of the 1947 Town and Country Planning Act, the profession became firmly entrenched within governmental bureaucracy. Thus, in addition to its own substantive goals, the profession was required to act in conformity with the norms of government service. Whilst it undoubtedly gained in influence through this 'marriage', it lost two important things in the process: its collective ability to criticise current policies and programmes from an independent viewpoint; and the credibility of its independence or influence as far as public opinion was concerned. Henceforth, public views and attitudes would be directed not to the planning profession, but to the political bosses who controlled them.

Secondly, the institutions of the welfare state, through their organisation and procedures, artificially severed the connections between physical and social concerns. The Ministry of Housing and Town Planning was concerned with the rebuilding of the physical fabric of the nation, while Ministries of Health, Pensions and National Insurance, Employment, and so on, healed its social ills. Unfortunately, these divisions persist to the present day and have resulted in town planning methods and techniques which are completely unable to take social issues into account.

Largely as a result of these two factors, the substantive content of planning has become conservative. Planners have found that it does not pay to be either idealistic, or overtly political. These modes of behaviour were ruled out, both through the restriction of planning to physical problems, and through accepted modes of British administrative behaviour. The identification of physical problems leads to the search for physical solutions, because planners do not, in the main, have access to other forms of solution. The Layfield Inquiry's critique of the Greater London Council's attempts to control office development and provide industrial jobs through floorspace controls and targets is a good example. How do planners induce the market to meet their targets without other substantial inducements or forms of control? Or again, the planners' response to high levels of juvenile delinquency or poverty in an area is to pull down the crowded terraces, and replace them with a new environment. But what are the planners to do when delinquency and poverty turn up on the new housing estates? It is an old planning tradition to equate aesthetic harmony with social harmony.

Two groups of people outside the planning field soon discovered that these physical solutions tended to cause underlying social problems to worsen rather than improve. One group, composed mainly of social scientists, discovered, for example, that expanded provision of council housing led to the deterioration of the private rented sector,[3] and thus to overcrowding and homelessness; that redevelopment led to the disruption of important social and cultural systems[4]; that industrial location policies decanted job opportunities to the suburbs and new towns, where those who needed them most could not gain access to them[5]; that urban motorways led to less public transport, thereby worsening the situation for those families without a car; and many other apparent inconsistencies inherent in the conventional planning wisdom.

These same facts were also discovered much earlier by another group – the workers and residents whom the planners identified as being ostensibly the beneficiaries of their policies. Their discovery was just a part of the changing fabric of their daily lives, however. In short, what the widespread and institutionalised application of planning expertise did was to hasten the emergence of a class in British society which, in one way or another, is systematically deprived of the benefits offered by social democracy. Planning has indeed come a long way from the optimistic beginnings of its utopian founders.

We have stated this critique at length for two reasons. Firstly, it is appropriate in a volume of this nature to question just what is meant by public service; and secondly, planning education in Britain is cast in the mould of a preparation for professional practice of the kind described here. The idea of community service in planning education therefore raises fundamental questions about the nature of the education itself.

While we have presented the critique in terms of Town Planning, we think it raises general questions relevant to all professions:

To what extent does identifying public service with private service lead to conservatism, rather than to innovative responses to social and environmental problems?

To what extent does this obscure the fact that such service is available to some sections of the public and not to others?

To what extent does the practitioner act in an individualistic way, and to what extent is he conscious of his membership in, or involvement with, a social group? To what extent does he render service as a private individual, and to what extent as a public citizen?

The elements of this critique have been known since at least 1958.[6] But positive responses have been slow in developing. We shall state the important elements of the response which goes furthest in developing lines for action and change, merely noting here that these are shared by only a small part of the profession as yet, although others may accept some of the supporting arguments. When these arguments are fully accepted, they form a new interpretation of the public service ideal.

Firstly, it is recognised that both market and governmental mechanisms operate in such a way as to deprive certain groups of access to, or influence over, public policy, of which town planning is a key part. This is clearly seen in the 'poverty and power' arguments.[7] The poor have little control or influence over market mechanisms, due to their low income. If, at the same time, the poor form only a minority within any kind of political constituency, they have little power in the electoral processes of democracy. They are, prima facie, excluded. When the analysis is extended to account for the interdependencies between political and economic power, even larger groups are excluded from influence over the processes which determine public policy.[8] Thus the first element in an alternative ideal is to postulate that such groups have a *fundamental* right to determine policy considerations, with the redistributive effects this implies – and specifically, a right to the direct, rather than indirect, services of planners.

Secondly, this response rejects all social and professional relationships based on the authority of expertise. This kind of authority in human relationships is closely related to the exercise of the kinds of social and economic power which are rejected by the ideal. However, there are also stronger reasons for rejecting the authority of expertise. Drawing heavily on adult education and community work experience, those who accept the alternative response feel that any kind of service which includes a sharp distinction between helper and helped will, in the long run, be detrimental to those helped. They argue that the distinction, when it forms part of daily relationships, tends to create or prolong a state of dependency which leads to alienation. Other conceptions of public service tend to overlook the fundamentally political nature of the planning job. What residents and workers in deprived areas need is not only access to the material benefits of modern society, but, more important in the longer term, access to, and influence over, the economic and political institutions which distribute those benefits.

At the same time, this approach emphasises an ideal of a group of *equals*, jointly discussing and determining courses of action. This kind of relationship is part of the aspiration of both liberal democracy and socialism, and has led recently to a focus on collaborative work with small groups and localised communities. Although the question must eventually be faced of how these ideas can be extended over wider areas of society, we believe that it is important to carry our knowledge and experience forward in those areas where new forms of co-operative action appear possible at the present time.

DEVELOPMENT OF AN ALTERNATIVE –
COMMUNITY PLANNING

If we are going to argue that this new interpretation of the public service ideal is relevant to professional practice today, we must show that it is feasible, and point out the ways in which it differs from traditional practice.

The most important function of any ideal is that it forms a coherent justification for the attitudes and procedures adopted by people in their everyday work. There is a presumption underlying many institutional and bureaucratic activities, that the substantive policies and programmes which arise out of the specialised attitudes and procedures adopted, are justifiable merely because they do so arise. Thus, we are saying, not only, that 'means' come to justify 'ends', but that the perpetuation of means (attitudes and procedures) becomes an end in itself. Whilst it is possible to reject an ideal either on grounds of the results it produces, or on the grounds that the procedures and attitudes it encourages are wrong, we focus our attention on attitudes and procedures because we see the problem as political, and believe that new (and we hope better) attitudes will not necessarily bring about new physical phenomena, but new modes of political determination.

This point can be demonstrated by a simple example. Neither the new nor the traditional interpretation of the ideal would question the need to provide adequate housing. Yet the practical interpretation of terms such as 'provide' and 'adequate' would be substantially different. The question of access to housing opportunities would also be dealt with quite differently – on the one hand through market and public sector mechanism, on the other through co-operative (and not necessarily municipal or state) forms of ownership and control.

In order to demonstrate further that the new interpretation is compatible with the essence of planning as a practical approach to collective policy, we have isolated three factors which are common to all types of planning. The form of the ideal we subscribe to can be expressed in terms of these factors, and the style which results can be designated 'community planning'.

There are many possible definitions and descriptions of planning, all of which are useful in different contexts. Often these definitions describe the kinds of outputs or goals pursued by the planners, or the objects planners manipulate in the course of their activities. There are three elements, however, which are implicit in all the possible definitions. The first is that all planning is orientated towards action. That is, one plans to *do* something, and the nature of this something determines the kind of planning that occurs. In community planning, the nature of the action is co-operative. The planner becomes one among a group, and the group determines the nature and extent of the planned action. In other words, he is definitely *not* standing in the traditional role of a consultant, being paid in cash or personal gratification simply for his expertise, which he superimposes upon the situation. To put it another way, his primary reference group is the group with whom he is working. It is neither other professionals, nor is it government service.

Secondly, all planning is concerned with the explicit pursuit of valued ends. In other words, planning aims to bring about conditions or events which have previously been determined to be of value. The question of *how* the values and ends are determined and applied in action is inescapable. In community planning, the traditional means of determining values and ends as reflected in contemporary political structures are questioned. There is no presumption that the appropriate ends are those espoused by a professional consensus. Nor, on the other hand, do these ends have to be those publicly espoused by government.

In addition, community planning is based on a different source of knowledge about community objectives and the political means of realising them. This knowledge arises out of interaction within the group or community and may never come to be specifically formulated. The planner in this situation learns less about goals from the formal communication of representatives than from sharing in, and empathising with, the needs and aspirations of the group as a whole.

This consideration merges with the third element of planning, which is that all planning is concerned with change of some kind – large or small, fundamental or marginal. Such changes always involve human values in choosing the ends pursued and almost always involve human behaviour, in one way or another. Where the connection with behaviour is direct, this connection is explicitly designated *social change*. Because of the way in which community planners derive their knowledge of values and ends, it follows that they must see social change as possible through effective group action, and not as an independent force to which the group can only adapt. In addition, the benefits brought about by this group action must not be attributed solely to the planner's own status or expertise, but to the group as a whole.

In conclusion, community planning is wider in scope than present forms of environmental or local government planning. It is not restricted to the concerns of any one agency or organisation, but is concerned with 'planning to meet the needs of the community within a specified area, irrespective of the particular organisation which might be involved – or even whether any organisation would be involved'.[9]

THE EDUCATION OF COMMUNITY PLANNERS

In the previous section, we argued that the ideal which underlies community planning, if it is to be implemented, requires certain kinds of attitudes on the part of its advocates and we identified three formative attitudes. Firstly, community planning demands a co-operative or collectivistic approach to action. Secondly, it sees the sources which determine the legitimate use of power as lying in group processes and interactions. Expertise, in and of itself, is not a legitimate source of power in community planning. Finally, we argue that the community planner must judge factual knowledge, not in terms of traditional academic criteria, but in terms of the salience and credibility of this knowledge to the community with whom he is working. That is, he must consider why, in political terms, certain kinds of factual knowledge are significant, while others are irrelevant.

All three of these attitudes pose serious problems for the teacher or institution which hopes to train community planners. Traditional approaches to education, and traditional attitudes of teachers, presume (to put it crudely) that because of his professional or academic qualifications, the teacher knows best! A related problem lies in the fact that many students entering planning schools have only recently left secondary or other forms of further education in which reciprocal attitudes have been reinforced – that is, students also assume that teacher knows best.

Changing the educational environment itself poses many of the same problems which community planning hopes to overcome in other environments. However, when a school becomes involved in ongoing community planning, an additional problem is raised. Not only at an individual level is there a problem of expertise, but *the institution itself becomes symbolic of power*, based on the accumulated knowledge and expertise of its members. Philosophically, knowledge is *not* power. Power derives from the codification and systematisation of knowledge that occurs within educational institutions, among other places. Thus, there is always the underlying feeling that the institution not only knows, but *knows best*. This kind of presumption is harder to break down than individual attitudes discussed previously, because it is symbolic and draws on deeply felt frustrations and aspirations within the community.

Thus, there are a number of inter-related problems of change which form the basis for further discussion: changing educational processes; changing political processes within a community and between that community and the larger society; and, based on these two, changing relationships between the educational institution and the community. In practice, distinct advantages are likely to arise because these changes are inter-related. Change in one sector, educational processes, can be made to ramify throughout both the educational institution and the community. Moreover, experience gained in the educational situation can be transferred to the community situation. Successful community planning experience in the field must be based firmly in this complexity – and indeed the nature of the educational problem makes it not only artificial, but actually dangerous, to discuss 'fieldwork' without discussion of the role it plays in bringing about these changes.

The general process of bringing about change in a social situation can be seen in the following way. Initially, a motivation for change must be created. Next, there must be an identification and selection of the kinds of changes that are desired, and finally, these changes must be built into the system in such a way that they persist over time, or until they are no longer appropriate.[10] Our focus in this paper is on the changes introduced into the educational environment, and the way in which related changes in the community and the educational institution are linked. While we emphasise the students' experience, how they are motivated and the way they are helped to identify possibilities for change, we have not attacked the associated problems of selection of particular changes or the way in which these changes are integrated into the student's personality. We feel that ultimately these kinds of decisions are not ours to make. They are properly decisions for each student to make for himself, in the light of his experience and development. To coerce students into these decisions, through the exercise of authority, would be just as wrong as similar coercion in the community.

PREPARATION FOR FIELDWORK

The initial stage of creating motivation for change involves two elements – the cognitive and the motivational. The cognitive element includes the student's view of the facts of social life within the school, and between the school and the community. The motivational aspect is concerned with his attitudes and procedures in interpreting these facts to determine appropriate courses of action for himself.

What are the facts of social life within the school, and how are they to be interpreted? Incoming students will tend to see the educational institution as merely a continuation of the sixth-form situation. There is a clear need for them to be 'de-schooled',[11] to develop attitudes toward, and expectations of, lecturers that are congruent with the attitudes involved in community planning. While this de-schooling process is most important at the beginning of a community planning course, it continues throughout. The first step involves the individual student identifying with the student body and, at the same time, understanding the importance of his own personality in group processes. To a large extent this is achieved through encouraging full group discussion of problems encountered either by the group as a whole, or by individual members of the group in activities based on his membership of the group. Individual problems are shared and are seen to reflect on the group as a whole. Eventually, the educational process comes to be socialised. Students begin to learn as much from each other – in discussion and argument – as they originally expected to learn only from the 'teaching staff'.

In order for this to occur, lecturers themselves must learn to be stubbornly non-authoritarian in their approach. Authority, where it is necessary, must be seen as serving to promote group formation. Other exercises of authority on the part of lecturers must come to be questioned by students. The lecturers must also be de-schooled. The process becomes co-operative and collaborative – both students and lecturers are aiming for the same goal, but each group has a particular and complementary role in achieving it. An indication of this process occurs when staff and students jointly determine criteria for assessment. Staff are seen as advising on general objectives; the student determines when these general objectives are relevant to either his own learning, or to the group's situation. Another indicator is collaboration between staff and students in determining an appropriate approach to, and organisation of, material to be covered in a particular area of study. Different groups of students have different problems which concern them, and different procedures for learning within the group. If students cannot communicate these to staff, neither will be able to achieve their aims.

These are perhaps simple and everyday problems. Yet, in working out solutions which are mutually satisfactory, a great deal is learned about day-today administration and organisation, which is also relevant to community planning. The substance of the problems may be different, but the processes of communication, sharing, co-operation, conflict resolution and consensus formation are general, and occur in any social group situation. They are also the informal processes on which any formal political action depends. To the extent that the student gains experience in these processes, consciously reflects on them, and begins to shape them as a member of a group, he is prepared for more difficult tasks to come.

Thus, authority relationships among staff and students are systematically altered. This alteration is justifiable on the grounds that it aids the *transfer of expertise from the professional to the non-professional,* in this case from teacher to student. At the same time, it may be explicitly or consciously taken to be a model for future situations in community planning, when the planner will be transferring his expertise to the community and developing his ideas in the light of their experiences.

However much the student may experience learning processes at this level, he must be led to reflect on them, by comparing them with similar processes elsewhere, and by being able to criticise them. Thus, an important part of the community planning course is to provide a framework for this criticism and comparison. This can be done using a number of complementary mechanisms. The factual material can be organised to emphasise both the diverse frames of reference possible in analysing the same phenomena, and the contemporary issues involved. Alternative analyses and strategies may be debated, and the debate focused around why different groups feel particular changes are necessary, and how other groups react to these proposals.

It must also be recognised that the subject matter itself, town planning, is not value free. As we indicated earlier, the practice of all planning involves trying to bring about a situation or an event which is itself valued. It is now largely accepted among planning educationalists that simply because of the nature of the subject matter, *planning education* cannot be value free. However, rather than simply accept that there is a difference between values and facts, the many kinds of connections between the two must be explored: the way in which the two sets of phenomena are inextricably linked in our daily language, in attitudes, biases, expectations and so on. These can be incorporated, for the sake of communication, in a model of planning activities, which stresses the role of formulating explicit criteria in evaluation, and attempting to relate these criteria to the fundamental goals and values which govern human situations and endeavour. In other words students are encouraged to express their own attitudes and biases, insofar as possible, since we believe that only when an individual is aware of his own attitudes is he able to take into account other people's values.

At the same time, students need a rigorous training in the nature of factual knowledge. A fair proportion of course work must be concerned with familiarising students with the traditional academic criteria governing the validity and reliability of knowledge, the methods by which factual information is gathered and the various philosophical positions which influence these procedures. This is done because only a thorough understanding of the *tentative* nature of factual knowledge gives one grounds for questioning the 'authority of expertise'. Students learn that most accepted wisdom is not only not disproven, but that it can never be positively proven.[12]

Through the mechanisms described above, the alteration of authority relationships and the organisation of course content, students are prepared for their first encounters in the field in community planning. This careful preparation is necessary for it will involve, to a greater extent than in most other types of community service we can think of, the student taking responsibility for the effects of his own actions on other people's lives. At the same time, he may undergo experiences which affect him deeply and to which he must respond positively and maturely.

THE BASIS FOR COMMUNITY FIELDWORK

Once students have been adequately prepared, they are ready to participate in community planning field work. But what must the school do in order to ensure that both the students and the community derive benefit from the field work?

There are probably few, if any, planning schools in Britain which do not now have at least some of their students involved with community service or community action work of some kind. Most often this is seen as being an unofficial and extra-curricular addition to the course by students as individuals, but some schools seem to be formalising their involvement with community groups within the course structure, as part of their education of students in line with 'participation requirements' of the planning legislation.[13]

These unofficial approaches probably generate as many problems for the community as they solve. The root of these problems lies in the unwillingness of the school, or educational institution as a whole, either to accept the goals or styles of action of the community, or to accept that, in field work, the student must be primarily responsible to the community, and responsible to the school only in a secondary sense. In other words, the school must willingly give up some of its *authority* over the student – recognising both the student's maturity and autonomy, and the autonomy of the community in defining its own goals. Nonetheless, the school is still *responsible* for the student's actions, if the ideal of co-operative action is to be sustained in practice.

It seems to us, therefore, that the relationship between the school and the community must be long-term. Community action in general is characterised by a necessity for both day-to-day continuity, and a spasmodic peaking of activity, the timing of which is often outside the community's control. Thus the school must accept that student activity will need to be programmed in terms of the scheduling of community-based activities, and not by the normal kind of academic timetable. At the same time, the long-term relationship with the community must be maintained, through staff members within the school. This continuous involvement is necessary to smooth out fluctuations in student involvement, and aids the ability of teaching staff within the school to assume responsibility not only for the direction and quality of the work done, but also for assisting with other elements of the community's programme, such as research and monitoring.

Which kinds of community should a school develop this kind of long-term relationship with? At the moment, there is very little experience on which to base a generalised answer to this question, although many will feel that the answer is obvious and the question redundant. On the one hand there is the argument that the schools should help those communities which need it most. On the other hand, it can be argued that immature students, particularly, should only be introduced in situations where there is a high level of experience already present within the community and where they can do least harm. In the meantime, the planning schools go on in an *ad hoc* way, and with little sharing of experience and ideas, while outside the planning schools, there are a number of initiatives being taken in an attempt to collate information and experience in community planning.

The Town and Country Planning Association, a voluntary organisation, has set up a 'Planning Aid Service' for community organisations. Since it cannot respond to all the requests for help it receives, the TCPA has decided to select its work on the basis, first, of working with groups who have *least* chance of obtaining advice elsewhere, and second, of achieving experience in as wide a variety of circumstances as possible. The Planning Exchange in Glasgow is likely to collect and co-ordinate similar information and experience in Scotland. The City Poverty Committee, drawing on George Clark's experience of community action in Notting Hill, is helping

H

to set up community planning programmes in collaboration with local groups in several parts of Britain. These will go further than the provision of occasional advisory services.

In the governmental sector, at both local and central levels, new approaches to planning are incorporating what is called the 'total approach' to urban problem solving. The Home Office, through its Urban Programme and particularly its community development projects, the Department of Health and Social Security in its own study of the 'poverty cycle', and through its initiative in reorganising local government social service departments; the Department of Education and Science in the Educational Priority Area schemes; the Department of the Environment's urban studies; and a number of city-sponsored projects; all demonstrate the search for new approaches to the problems of urban Britain.

Other initiatives, from both the voluntary and government sectors, can be expected over the next few years. It is to this new phenomenon of widespread, positive discrimination that the planning schools need to turn their attention. In the early stages, indeed, their direct involvement with community planning may occur through co-operation with such agencies.

Meanwhile, we stress simply that when students do fieldwork in community planning, there must be strong and continuing contact between the school and the community, and that the school, the community organisation, and the students must carefully work out beforehand the principles which will govern the students' involvement and the kinds of tasks which the students will undertake initially. The irresponsibility of failing to prepare in this manner is demonstrated in the case of the London college which sent out its students to conduct a doorstep survey of household characteristics and housing conditions. It happened that in the area to which they were sent, the community organisation had simultaneously announced a similar exercise of its own. The students came into the area without first making contact with anyone in the community and were initially amazed by the high level of co-operation they 'achieved'. It was not until families realised that the students had nothing to do with the survey they were expecting that some of them complained to the college, and the students were called off. By that time, it was too late to start the community's own survey, because many families didn't understand why they needed to be interviewed again so quickly. Thus, the community programme was set back by several months, and this could have been politically disastrous. There was serious talk of non-cooperation with academic institutions in the future.

Following adequate preparation, how is the student introduced into the community, so that he comes, through his *own* experiences, to gain an understanding of the community and its members? The answer to this question depends on the way the community groups are organised and their stage of development. Many such organisations are faced with a chronic shortage of funds and personnel, so that they must rely on the help of 'outsiders' and must face the question of how to train and integrate such people into the appropriate procedures for coping with their problems. In this context, the Notting Hill Housing Service serves as a good example of how a community organisation can be structured to achieve its own goals, while meeting the need to train volunteers.

The Notting Hill Housing Service was one of the earliest voluntary organisations concerned with community planning, and produced the widely cited report on housing conditions in North Kensington in 1969.[14] Its programme was designed to work at three different levels: it sought to help individuals and families within the community; to work with existing and newly forming community and neighbourhood organisations which would take up the wider policy issues affecting families in the area; and in addition, it was concerned with testing approaches and solutions which might have wider applicability in community planning. Like many other organisations in the voluntary sector, it was often short of funds for permanent staff and therefore used students in a number of different ways in its work.

The Service discovered very early that, apart from simple tasks, people from outside the area could not be really useful to either the organisation or the community until they had undergone a period of acclimatisation in North Kensington, or had gained experience in similar areas. For this reason, it usually refused to accept students 'on placement' for less than a three-month period, and preferred even longer association.

The initial acclimatisation of students involves intensive briefing sessions. These have two purposes: to get to know the community, its specific problems, personalities, internal and external relationships; and to identify, as precisely as possible, not only the ways in which students can be of benefit to the community, but also, and more important, to spell out those ways in which students can do harm in the area. The second of these is particularly important for planning and architecture students, most of whom have had no previous education in social or behavioural science.

Students joining the organisation should be encouraged to spend a short time 'getting to know' the area and the community organisations, without any specific work tasks being assigned for them. At the same time they may attend meetings and working sessions, and take part in discussions and seminars of their own, and informally meet and talk with key people in the neighbourhood.

Following this briefing period, students can be further integrated into the community, through performing routine but essential tasks within the organisation. Typical jobs range from researching the current level of rent being set by rent officers and tribunals, helping in the reception of people coming to the organisation for help or advice, to helping with arrangements for neighbourhood meetings and leafleting in the community. These jobs further introduce the student to the people and problems within the area.

Even at this level of activity, some students find that proximity to family and community problems is too painful an experience for them. In these circumstances, students either withdraw from the community or find different tasks which are not so personally involving. In addition, there may be instances where the personality or style of an individual does not fit well with the nature of the work, and it is necessary to redefine his work tasks, to take him away from areas of sensitivity.

Thus, the introduction of students to straightforward and simple tasks acts as an important check on their preparation and ability, before they are committed irretrievably to more sensitive work. It also gives them an opportunity to accept, and be accepted by, the people with whom they work. Most will then be able to move into more difficult areas of work, requiring some personal skill on their part. In terms of the Housing Service's programme, students were able to move from doing essential back-up work, into areas requiring the exercise of mature judgement and sensitivity. Even so, all students worked under the supervision of a permanent member of the group.

The nature of the Housing Service's work entailed students accompanying families to administrative hearings concerned with rents, security of tenure, welfare rights and the work of local authority departments in general. Students may also work with different kinds of community and neighbourhood organisations and be concerned with planning, education, housing, the environment, old people, teenagers and so on. In each of these areas, students can make an effective contribution to the community programme and, depending on the ability of the individuals concerned, progress to community planning work of a high standard.

What happens when the student has completed his fieldwork experience? We have stressed throughout that while the student is in the field, his primary responsibility is to the community. If, however, the fullest possible learning use is to be made of the experience, it must be further discussed when the student returns to the formal educational environment. Here, he will be encouraged to reflect on his experience and to analyse critically his own performance in the field, with a view to identifying both his strengths and weaknesses. Students who have been working in different communities can compare and contrast their experiences and discuss the efficacy of different approaches and solutions. Ultimately, they will develop their own ideas and theories of community planning, theories which must include an assessment of their own role as community planners.

We have remarked earlier that tendencies in this direction already exist within many planning schools, and that the major problem which confronts planning schools is the 'political' nature of any direct involvement with community planning. A common way to solve this problem is for the planning school to set up a classroom-orientated project around a community planning problem and invite representatives of the local authority, local interests and community organisations to 'teach-ins' and briefing sessions. The students then carry out traditional field-study exercises, surveys and investigations, return to the classroom and draw up a scheme or programme. Representatives of the community are then invited back for their views on what has been produced. As an extension of the traditional 'studio project' in planning or architecture, this is clearly an interesting way of exposing students to new ideas and contacts, but achieves little in the way of channelling their effort into the real situation, as it does little to challenge the planner's traditional view of his role and relationship with 'the planned'. Even when students in this situation are invited to show their work to other members of the community, as sometimes happens, little has been done which changes this traditional relationship. It is still the professional's analysis and solutions which are on offer.

A second method of involving students in community planning situations is for the school and community organisation to set up a joint project, which attempts to satisfy educational objectives, by employing students in set tasks for a limited period of time within the context of the community's own programme. In this way, students may become involved in survey work within the community; researching planning, housing or development issues as information back-up to community discussion and policy-making. On occasions, students may even help prepare planning briefs and studies for the community's future.

While this approach has considerable advantages over classroom exercises, in that students work from within or alongside the community organisation structure and are, therefore, more likely to make a contribution to the community programme, it too suffers from the disadvantage that students can consider the experience merely an extension of their classroom studies. Students still see their primary responsibility as being to the school rather than to the community. There is, therefore, little reason for them to change their view of their future professional role.

On the basis of the experience of a number of planning schools over the past few years, we, therefore, argue strongly for the approach to community planning fieldwork experience which we have developed in this paper.

CONCLUSION

In this paper we have chosen to direct our attention to an ideal of public service, rather than to the more specfic concept of community service. Why? We feel that discussing community service in planning education carries with it the connotation of extending current problems, inherent in practice, into the fieldwork experience. Because much of planning is built on the model of private consultancy, such an approach can lead merely to new forms of consultancy which perpetuate the helper-helped dichotomy. Undoubtedly, even within traditional planning courses, this kind of fieldwork can affect students greatly and lead eventually to more politically open forms of planning in future. But we have two reservations about such fieldwork. On the one hand, there is a world of difference between a traditional planner being sensitised to the aspirations of localised groups and a planner who is actively working with these groups to promote their own political self-determination. On the other hand, we feel that there is a need for acknowledging *now* the fundamentally political nature of planning, and for educating young planners who can work fully and effectively within this political framework in the near future. Planning is at the crossroads and the decision must be made. For current urban programmes to be effective, the professionals who staff them will need to have positive attitudes towards, and abilities in, co-operative politics. The development of these attitudes and abilities is too important to be left to chance processes within traditionally orientated courses.

Community planning must be seen not as an extension of the planner's traditional field of practice, but as part of a wider process of community development and political change.

A new approach to education is required in order to do this. This approach will have, as its primary function, not only the education of a non-elitist professional group, but also a significant contribution to the education of the public, to help identify some of the levers of change through which communities can improve their quality of life.

REFERENCES

1 Edgar H. Schein, *Professional Education: Some New Directions*, McGraw Hill, London, 1972.
2 Donald L. Foley, 'Britain Town Planning: One Ideology or Three?' *British Journal of Sociology*, vol 11, 1960. Reprinted in Andreas Faludi (ed) *A Reader in Planning Theory*, Pergamon Press, Oxford, 1973.
3 Michael Dear, 'Housing Projections for London', *Quarterly Bulletin*, Intelligence Unit, Greater London Council, no. 14, March 1971.
4 Peter Willmott and Michael Young, *Family and Kinship in East London*, Routledge & Kegan Paul, London, 1958.
5 D. W. Rowbotham, *The Decentralisation of Industry from Inner London*, unpublished thesis, Department of Social and Environmental Planning, Polytechnic of Central London, May 1971.
6 Ruth Glass, 'The Evaluation of Planning: Some Sociological Considerations', *International Social Science Journal*, vol XI, no. 3, 1959. Reprinted in Faludi, op. cit.
7 Peter Willmot and Michael Young, op. cit.
8 C. Wright Mills, *The Power Elite*, Oxford University Press, London, 1956.
9 J. D. Stewart, 'Community and Corporate Planning in Two Tier Local Government', *Journal of the Royal Institute of Town Planning*, September/October 1972.
10 Edgar H. Schein, 'The Mechanisms of Change', in Bennis, Schein, Steele and Berlew (eds) *Interpersonal Dynamics*, Homewood, Illinois: The Dorsey Press, 1964. An abridged version is reprinted in Warren

B. Bennis, Kenneth C. Benne and Robert Chin (eds) *The Planning of Change*, second edn, Holt, Rinehart and Winston, Inc., London, 1969.

11　Ivan Illich, *Deschooling Society*, Penguin Books, Harmondsworth, 1973.

12　Karl R. Popper, 'On the Sources of Knowledge and Ignorance', in *Conjectures and Refutations*, fourth edn, Routledge & Kegan Paul, London, 1972.

13　Report of the Committee on Public Participation in Planning, *People and Planning* (The Skeffiington Report), HMSO, London, 1969.

14　Notting Hill Housing Service, *Notting Hill Housing Survey*, 1969.

Chapter Six

Community - related Project Work in Engineering

BY JOHN BROWN AND SINCLAIR GOODLAD

Professor John Brown is Head of the Department of Electrical Engineering at the Imperial College of Science and Technology, London University. From 1962–5, he was professor of Electrical Engineering and Dean of Engineering at the Indian Institute of Technology, Delhi. Between 1970 and 1971, he was Chairman of the Electronics Division of the Institution of Electrical Engineers, and between 1972 and 1973 Deputy Chairman of its Education and Training Committee. He is author of *Microwave Lenses*, 1955, *Radio Surface Waves* (with H. M. Barlow), 1962, and *Telecommunications* (revised edition with E. V. D. Glazier), 1973.

Sinclair Goodlad (biographical notes with the Introduction) is responsible for the Group Project scheme for engineering students described in this chapter.

This chapter explores the possible combination of educational and social objectives in interdisciplinary project work, which is the sort of study most likely to give engineering students the chance to engage themselves with problems of the socially underprivileged. It examines: some of the uses made of individual and group project work in undergraduate studies; the commitment of time by staff and students relative to that required for other types of study; the academic and social objectives of project work; factors leading to success or failure in projects; and the benefits and difficulties found in individual and group project work. Illustrations of community-related projects are given from a scheme of group projects undertaken by electrical engineering students at Imperial College.

The argument is conducted primarily in terms of the educational benefits likely to accrue to students, because if educational innovation does not meet this fundamental requirement it will not commend itself to institutions of higher education and will not be of ultimate benefit to society. This assessment of the strengths and weaknesses of individual and group project work, as a form of engineering education, should be of value to those in engineering education who would like to see a more vigorous linking of curriculum and service. It should also suggest to those in the 'front line' of community service and community action what sort of practical help it is reasonable to request from engineering departments.

To a certain extent, all engineering involves the systematic application of knowledge to meet human need. What distinguishes the humane application of technical knowledge in community service from other applications of knowledge? It can be argued, and indeed *has* often been argued, that what an engineer does with his technical knowledge is his own concern, and that it is no business of institutions of higher education to do anything other than supply him with the necessary knowledge and skill with which to get a job. The choice of job will reflect the individual's specific interests and talents and his ideological predilections. The humaneness or otherwise of a man's activity will reflect the degree of his social as well as technical enlightenment and his compassion. Against this, it has been argued that the professional is a man who not only knows a technique, but understands the situations in which that technique would be appropriate. That is to say, he does not simply apply technical knowledge at other people's behest, but rather makes independent judgements about a situation, with due understanding of political, economic, social, and other purposes.

Much engineering is nowadays carried out in large organisations, where the individual engineer may be many times removed from the front line. He is likely to be involved in highly specialised tasks of analysis, design, etc. without necessarily having personal experience of the social pressures which determine the specifications to which he is asked to work. If, therefore, he is to exhibit the informed detachment implicit in his role of professional, it is appropriate that he has at least thought through the factors which render his particular application of knowledge humane or otherwise. It follows that his education should have equipped him to do this. At what stage in the engineer's professional education (which of course takes place outside educational institutions as well as inside them) is enlightenment about technique to be fused with enlightenment about the social situations in which technique can be applied? And where is the young engineer to get personal experience of work which exposes him to the social, political, economic and other pressures which influence his application of technical knowledge and which are in turn influenced by it?

The commercial processes of private industry may result in the production of goods or services which meet human needs. Indeed, the humane benefits to the socially underprivileged resulting from industrial processes may be of the highest concern to the shareholders who own the industry. But, typically, the work of private industry is described primarily in terms of profitability, growth, etc. Similarly, in government work, engineering activity may have no immediate visibility in terms of direct human application. With funds drawn from taxation, only such diffuse concepts as public accountability mediate between policy and practice. The young engineer may find himself isolated from the needs which arouse his compassion by several layers of administration.

However, in addition to commercial and government enterprise, one can identify a growing area of 'voluntary' activity. The word 'voluntary' does not signify that the 'volunteers' necessarily work for nothing; it suggests, rather, that the work carried out is inspired not by commercial motive, nor by statute, but by the social, political, ideological or other commitment of small or large groups. Money may come from the general public not in return for commercial services or goods, nor in the form of taxation, but as donations to trusts, subscriptions to charities, etc. dedicated to the furtherance of some ideology or humane objective. The many conservation organisations are examples of such initiative. In this sort of context, as indeed in a small business, it is clearly possible for the engineer to see not only the source of his funds, but also the application of his ideas in small-scale situations.

Engineering work relevant to commercial and government organisations can, of course, be carried out by students either inside or outside institutions of higher education. Through sponsored research and consultancy, a considerable degree of flexibility is possible at postgraduate level. The interests of 'voluntary' organisations can be catered for in like manner. In all these cases, the benefit is mutual: the outside interest gains from the detached scholarship of the educational institution and the educational institution fertilises its theoretical preoccupations with practical problems. Postgraduate students learn to apply knowledge as they acquire it. And although the problems considered in this way in universities arise from pressing political, social, and other concerns, universities are committed to detachment – the dispassionate consideration of available options. A wide range of possibilities can be considered in any situation – not just the ones likely to earn quick money or free a political log-jam. In this context, humane considerations can at least be heard and judged.

Granted that the humane application of knowledge in community service is a concept relevant to, and possible in, postgraduate education, is it relevant also in *undergraduate* education? Can undergraduate engineering education not only provide that involvement with social issues which is a necessary part of the professional engineer's training, but also provide a means for applying knowledge and skill to practical problems?

Research, which is the most obvious point of contact between university engineering and the defined needs of other institutions, can take two major forms: firstly, the creation of new knowledge, new that is not only to the client, but also to the engineering profession; secondly, the spreading around, re-arranging and interpretation and dissemination of fundamental theory for application to particular problems arising from practical requirements. The first activity, the creation of new knowledge, is most readily acceptable in universities because it is the activity of highest prestige and provides the greatest career potential in the present university ethos and structure. Where promotion depends largely on the number of papers published, on the legitimation of intellectual concepts and discoveries by professional peers, there is a ready incentive to undertake work which not only meets the needs of outside organisations, but also contributes to the process of publishing to avoid perishing. Happily, there is still a strong tradition of consultancy and independent service in applying existing knowledge to specific practical problems. This form of 'research' activity is particularly important as it impinges upon the instruction of undergraduates. Where existing knowledge has to be applied to a novel problem, the possibilities of involving undergraduates are great. Knowledge does not need to be new to the engineering profession to be new to undergraduates! Indeed, there is some value in knowledge not being new because, like new wine, knowledge needs time to mature. When all knowledge within limits of comparable intellectual difficulty is new, it does not matter, intellectually, what one strives to understand; it does, however, matter considerably, from the point of view of morale at least, for engineering students to *feel* that one has the opportunity to apply knowledge as one acquires it, to *situations* which are new.

The involvement of undergraduates in the process of applying knowledge as they acquire it requires work in the form of projects, rather than as set experiments associated with a traditional course of lectures, seminars, tutorials, etc. When the criteria of effectiveness in the application of knowledge are determined by real human situations, and not by ideal conditions laid down by the 'discipline', such projects must be interdisciplinary ones.

The present discussion of the concept of the humane application of knowledge in community service, as it applies in engineering education, will concentrate on a scheme of interdisciplinary group projects carried out by electrical engineering students at Imperial College. The combination in this work of academic and social objectives suggests considerable possibilities for future work. But because interdisciplinary group project work is not the only sort of project work carried out in university engineering departments, a preliminary comparison will be made with other types of project work found in undergraduate engineering studies. The information used in support of the points made in this chapter is based largely on a study of project work in Imperial College, carried out by Dr Sinclair Goodlad, Dr Gwyn Thomas, and Mr Damian Cummins. In a constantly changing situation, it is inappropriate to give detailed facts and figures, but the study provides a useful, qualitative picture of the benefits and drawbacks of project work in engineering.

TYPES OF PROJECT WORK: POSSIBLE AND ACTUAL

Many different types of project work are possible in engineering studies at undergraduate level. These include:

1 Pieces of research work carried out in the laboratory or in the field or by theoretical developments, where the results are unkown both to the student and to the member of staff supervising the project work.

2 The solution of a scientific problem, which connects several topics within one discipline, drawn from different subjects, which have been studied previously. Such work may require experiment, calculation and design; the answer is unknown to the student, though the general lines of the solution may be known to the supervisor.

3 The design of a novel system or structure, of which there is no other example that can be copied, and which has a specification of such an unusual kind that a student must go back to the first principles of his discipline to solve it. The outcome is, thus, unknown to the supervisor, though he knows the criteria by which the solution may be judged. Design and make projects are an important category here. (See Allen, 1968,[1] and Allen, 1972.[2]) Other projects may require the design of a system or structure which does not necessarily have any novel features or unusual requirements, but where real restrictions are placed on it. Such designs can be carried out under 'codes of practice' and may call for a demonstration that the student knows his way around complex documents or routine procedures (in a student's own discipline or in another discipline).

4 A detailed study or planning investigation, which uses data that have been acquired by other people and of which the results are proposals or speculations. Clearly, there can be no direct check by student or supervisor that the scheme will work out in practice.

5 A review of a field of study, drawing together information and ideas from a wide range of bibliographic and other sources, showing how it forms a connected picture, and applying it to the consideration of a particular problem. The result may be a dissertation by an individual or by a group.

6 A study of a problem which is presented in vague terms, where the student has to identify subsidiary questions in one or more disciplines, which are capable of solution, and specify suitable methods of inquiry – whether or not he is able to carry out the inquiry himself in the time he has available.

At Imperial College, project work, typically, is carried out by individual students and is primarily 'technical' – that is to say not involving economic, social, political or other factors. The scheme of group projects to be discussed later differs in that it involves *groups* of students and is specifically designed to involve consideration of *external* criteria.

TIME DEVOTED TO PROJECT WORK BY STUDENTS AND BY STAFF

The time required for project work is of critical importance, not only because projects which are too time-consuming may be unacceptable in a crowded undergraduate degree programme, but also because a disproportionately heavy commitment of time by staff to project work, compared to time devoted to other types of teaching, may effectively deter staff from adopting project methods of teaching. Many discussions of teaching methods and of curricula are rendered utterly unintelligible by failure to specify the amount of time in anything other than vague references to 'terms' or 'years'. For ease of comparison, it will, therefore, be assumed that the undergraduate year consists of thirty weeks, with a notional forty hours of study per week, that is, 1,200 hours per year. Clearly, emphasis must be on the *notional* value of this – because a clever student will complete a given quantity of work in a shorter time and a less able student will probably spend substantially more time on the same work. However, there is some merit in having a uniform standard of reference.

At Imperial College, project work is, typically, undertaken in the third year of the undergraduate course. Civil and electrical engineers, for example, spend about one third of their total time in the third year on project work, while mechanical engineers spend about one quarter. Some projects are designed to occupy only one week (forty hours) or two weeks (eighty hours). By contrast, geology and mining geology students may devote half their total time to project work.

The amount of time devoted to any individual project will depend upon the type of work and what is to be achieved. Other factors, like the balance of total studies (to be reviewed below), will suggest appropriate balances between project work and other types of work. For group project study of engineering questions involving social, political, economic and other factors, a figure of approximately 100 hours of student study has been found suitable; in this time, students can gain a reasonably comprehensive picture of a question. If their work is to have some direct social utility, a figure of perhaps 150 hours might be appropriate.

To compare different types of project with one another, and project teaching with other types of teaching, we asked Imperial College staff to estimate the total supervision time for a project in lecturer-hours per student. For example, if one lecturer devoted a total of ten hours – tutorial, laboratory supervision, assessment, etc. – to a group of ten students on a project, the figure would be *one* lecturer-hour per student. It transpired that in Imperial College very large amounts of time indeed were devoted to individual students in the course of a project. Several projects involved more than ten lecturer-hours per student and one project involved forty-six hours per student. Naturally, field-work supervision in some subjects (for example, geology) involves considerable staff commitment in vacation time. In absolute terms, this may seem a great deal; but it is necessary to take into account the proportion of a student's total work-load the project involves and then to compare the staff time involved with the time which has to be devoted to other types of teaching – lecturing, tutoring, laboratory supervision. Again, some assumptions are helpful – even if the pressure on universities to increase 'productivity' is even now rendering the figures suspect! If it is assumed that one lecturer is responsible for the total education of fifteen students, and that each lecturer has a maximum of fifteen hours contact with students per week, then one lecturer could afford to devote one full hour each week to each student. Assume, too, that each student is expected to work for forty hours a week; a ratio can be established of one hour of staff time to forty hours of student work. If this one hour:forty hour ratio is taken as a reference level, it becomes possible to compare the effort expended in supervision of different kinds of work.

From such calculations, it was established that at Imperial College project work involved something like three times the commitment of staff time that might be expected from the 1:40 ratio calculated above. Such heavy demands on staff time were, it must be noted, involved primarily with projects which comprised laboratory work. All laboratory projects, of course, place a loading on laboratory technical staff – a factor which further diminishes the economy of effort involved.

It is, however, important to note that this comparison is limited to time spent. If the time is used more effectively than in other work, in activity which is intensely interesting and gives deep satisfaction to both staff and students, *real* efficiency may in fact be greater than in, say, a conventional lecture course, with tutorials and three-hour examinations. Concepts of 'productivity' in academic activity must be handled with caution.

SOME ACADEMIC OBJECTIVES OF PROJECT WORK

Proposals for combining academic and social objectives in projects concerned with the humane application of technical knowledge to community needs will be the more likely to succeed if they do not do violence to existing practice. Existing practice is not worth preserving in all detail; but it seems wise to proceed on the assumption that evolution is more likely to commend itself to academics than revolution.

In the study of project work at Imperial College, staff were offered for consideration an extensive list of general objectives and were asked to indicate which of them they thought applied to the project work they supervised. They were also asked to state, in their own words, any specific objectives of their own. The list was based upon the *Taxonomy of Educational Objectives: Handbook 1, Cognitive Domain* by B. S. Bloom *et al.* and the *Taxonomy of Educational Objectives: Handbook 2, Affective Domain* by D. R. Krathwohl *et al.* (both published by Longmans, London, 1956). These taxonomies rank educational objectives in each domain in ascending order of abstraction.

The Cognitive Taxonomy deals with knowledge, abilities, and skills, the Affective with attitudes. In the transmission of knowledge, the first type of educational activity deals with terminology; the next with sources of information; the third with specific facts and so on, up to the major unifying ideas in the subject – the theories and generalisations by which knowledge is organised. Similarly, the fundamental type of ability in a subject is that of comprehension, which is recognised by the student's ability to translate information from one level of abstraction to another; to interpret a communication, recognising essentials, unwarranted conclusions, etc.; to extrapolate, etc. Still higher in the levels of abstraction are placed the application of knowledge in practical instances; the analysis of ideas into their constituent parts; the synthesis of ideas, knowledge, etc. into unique communications, plans, sets of abstract relations, physical objects, etc. Finally, there is the ability to evaluate ideas, methods, etc. for some specific purpose, in terms not only of internal evidence – such as logical accuracy and consistency – but in terms of external criteria such as efficiency, economy, utility, social effects, and political consequences. This type of ability in evaluation, Bloom and his colleagues argue, is likely to be found in the most advanced activities of a profession.

The Affective Taxonomy ranks attitudes (and appreciation) from simple awareness of the existence of certain ideas, concepts, etc. through responding to and valuing them, to characterisation of the individual by a complex of values. Krathwohl and his colleagues attempt to rank attitudes from, for example, simply being aware of what engineers do to being a professional engineer in the most

I

complex and sophisticated understanding of the word professional.

Clearly, the more complex and ambitious the educational activity, the more objectives will it involve from the higher (more abstract) end of the taxonomies. And as the higher objectives embrace the others, it would not be surprising to find that an activity which placed, for example, evaluation of an idea as its principal objective also includes a wide range of other, lower objectives.

In discussing the project work of their respective departments, our colleagues indicated practically every objective as being suitable. However, a few points merit comment.

Firstly, several project supervisors specifically mentioned knowledge of library resources under 'Sources of Information' in the knowledge objectives of their projects. It seems that many projects are specifically designed to give students experience of carrying out a literature search, and some departments associate lectures on the use of libraries with their project activities.

Secondly, while several supervisors did not specifically mention knowledge objectives (and did not offer replies to the questions put to them about the ones on the list), ability and skill objectives were extensively mentioned. So too were attitude objectives. It is clear that projects are frequently regarded as the most 'professional' of a student's undergraduate studies in engineering.

Thirdly, it is interesting to note that although several projects required students to evaluate ideas, etc. in terms of the external criteria of efficiency and economy and utility, relatively few required students to consider the social effects or political consequences of particular activities. These objectives are likely to be legitimate and important ones in interdisciplinary engineering projects concerned with the humane application of knowledge; insofar as these objectives are included, these projects represent for most departments a significant departure from normal practice.

Fourthly, a few supervisors specifically repudiated knowledge objectives as being of primary concern in undergraduate studies. One tutor, concerned with a second-year laboratory-based project said 'The technical content is only the vehicle of the methodology.' At the relatively complex level of activity of final-year project work in a university engineering course, specific knowledge may be less important than generalised skills. One might even say that it does not matter what specific knowledge a student gains, provided that the gaining of that knowledge involves him in the exercise of skills which will be valid in his chosen profession.

Some of the specific objectives of interdisciplinary group project work in engineering will be discussed below. Meanwhile, it is necessary to confront perhaps the most difficult aspect of project work in engineering education: assessment.

THE ASSESSMENT OF STUDENTS AND THE EVALUATION OF PROJECTS

A necessary part of any academic enterprise is the method of seeing whether the objectives set have been achieved. In addition, there is the added burden of having to grade students – to rank them in order for the purposes of degree classification. This latter task should not be confused with the former; it is largely forced upon universities by students themselves (who seem inordinately keen on getting a meal ticket at the end of their studies) and by employers and grant-awarding authorities.

Project work is particularly difficult to assess, especially when different projects are being undertaken by different students. As anyone in education knows, it is difficult enough to assess achievement in standard tasks, let alone in tasks which differ one from the other. It is hard enough to compare one project with another in terms of the comparative difficulty and the standards expected to be achieved in each; it is even more difficult when one tries to assess the contribution of individual students to a group effort. For example, in a project group there may be one student who is particularly fertile in good ideas but who is relatively uncritical; another student may have no original ideas of his own, but may contribute significantly to the work of the group by ruthless scepticism and penetrating criticism of ideas put up by others. Another student may be a good 'front' man – skilled in penning a persuasive letter or in cajoling information from reluctant institutions on the telephone; another may not be good at any of these things, but systematic and methodical in pursuing and noting library information. All students in a group experience the pressures arising from the dynamic which groups have, and they may be more or less successful in overcoming some of the problems which arise. Typically, project work, if successful, will result in students being better informed on detail than their supervisors; there is obviously a problem here in that the supervisor may have considerable difficulty in checking the detailed accuracy of statements.

In the face of so many difficulties, what is to be done? An extreme

I*

suggestion bandied about in common rooms these days is that universities should cease to give degrees and simply report on what a student has done. This would throw the burden of decision onto students and onto their employers who would then be forced to ask detailed questions of the students and carry out any tests necessary to their own interests. After all, it can be argued, a student will not climb a cliff until he is sure that he knows enough about mountaineering technique to avoid killing himself; why then should he not be required to exercise similar judgement about his fitness to undertake skilled employment in highly technical work?

Granting that this idea may be too radical for most people, there is a reasonable compromise suggested by L. R. B. Elton (1968).[4] Elton's scheme, which is a sophistication of similar schemes common in American universities, is to attach a credit rating to an academic activity as a measure not of student achievement, but of the difficulty of the activity: the credit would be awarded if the student achieved a 'pass' mark in the activity. In addition to credit units, marks would be awarded – the number of marks reflecting the *reliability* with which the activity could be graded, the number of *credits* reflecting the validity of the enterprise in terms of the academic objectives of the course.

Whatever scheme finds favour, it is to be noted that any project work involving the humane application of knowledge which is to find favour in present circumstances in British universities must take cognisance of the responsibility which universities currently have for grading students, as well as assessing the achievement of students.

The evaluation of projects carried out by undergraduates raises a host of even more thorny questions. If project work involving front-line contact with the community is not to be a luxury for students, designed to give them deeper satisfaction in their studies, but is to be genuinely productive of social benefit, a way must be devised for ensuring that projects have the greatest possible likelihood of giving satisfaction on all counts. There may, for example, be better ways of finding a solution to a community's technical problems than having undergraduates sharpening their teeth on them. However, in the absence of other ways of dealing with the problems, there may be singular advantage in giving students their head, especially if doing so provides fertilisation of academic studies. At present, the means of evaluating the worth of projects, even within the university context, are rudimentary in the extreme; so many criteria come to bear when one tries to evaluate projects by undergraduates in a wider social context than at present, that it must be confessed, faith, hope and charity are more helpful than operational research.

All this being said, it is possible to point to a few features of individual and group projects which have led to success or the opposite. Naturally, success is primarily determined by the students involved. Enthusiasm and ability, like good actors in a bad play, can achieve wonders. But some factors intrinsic to the specific projects bear mention.

Firstly, successful projects have been found by many supervisors to be ones for which a suitable quantity of relevant published material exists. Unsuccessful projects have sometimes been ones launched into a relatively new field, for which there is little published information and where students have got lost. This bears out the point made earlier that, while a research-oriented faculty may favour knowledge which is new to the profession, knowledge which is new only to students may be most appropriate for project work.

Secondly and similarly, if the results of the project are entirely unknown (in outline as well as detail) to the supervisor, work can be too uncertain for students who are working to close time limits.

Thirdly, doubt has been cast on the value of projects which involve a large amount of repetition of standard techniques, or which require designs which only involve the application of codes of practice and which do not give students some practice in deciding broad outline.

Fourthly, projects have occasionally turned out to be too trivial or too difficult for students to achieve satisfaction in the time available. Clearly, one of the hardest tasks of the supervisor is to determine the appropriate scale of an activity of this sort.

The last two points suggest that if a project in the humane application of knowledge is to be successful in academic terms, it must be intellectually challenging as well as socially useful.

ACADEMIC AND PRACTICAL DIFFICULTIES EXPERIENCED WITH TRADITIONAL PROJECTS

Before we consider specific features of projects concerned with the humane application of knowledge in community service, it is valuable to review briefly some of the typical difficulties experienced with traditional projects in engineering courses. The following list is based upon replies given to the inquiry on projects in Imperial College. The number and type of difficulties experienced in any one project, as well as the intensity with which the difficulty was experienced, clearly depend upon a wide variety of factors. In contemplating new types of activity, it is, however, valuable to know in advance some of the difficulties one is likely to be up against.

1   Following on from what was noted in the previous section, there is the difficulty for supervisors of selecting suitable projects for the time available – whether the time is a few hours or a few weeks.

2   Occasionally there was an unexpected 'bug' in a problem – apparatus that failed to work for some unforeseeable reason, or, on one dreadful occasion, the theft from the university of a crucial piece of apparatus on the day before final readings were to be taken.

3   Sometimes technical support proves a problem. With experimental projects, there is the difficulty of getting enough apparatus and getting it in time. With some design and make projects in engineering, there is the problem of getting a large amount of student work through already overworked workshops – particularly when a very large number of students bring work along simultaneously.

4   Concentration on a project inevitably means a contraction in breadth of practical experience with standard experiments. Not only can a student fail to gain experience of standard experimental procedures, he can also, through concentrating on project work, remain ignorant of pieces of apparatus in everyday use in places where he is likely to seek employment. This problem may not be crippling; it must be foreseen.

5   Several supervisors at Imperial College mentioned a tendency of students to get too involved with their project work and to spend a disproportionate amount of time on it. This can be the tendency with the best students, who may thereby suffer in the degree assessment, when only a proportion of degree marks are allocated to any given activity.

6   Project work can be a traumatic experience for students who have all their lives been given specific tasks to carry out. Such students may find it difficult to work on their own and particularly to carry out work which is ill-defined. Whatever merits 'culture-shock' may have, its confusing effects on students and their subsequent degree performance must be foreseen.

7 Occasionally there has been incompatibility of students working in a group. In one group, a student of singular ability was not in sympathy with the objectives of the project and cast doubts on every suggestion volunteered by his colleagues – with damaging effect on morale. In another group, two students who did not get on well did not even know each other's names at the end of the year!

8 Individual technical projects are frequently designed to give a student his first contacts with research work. Faculty members offer to supervise projects within their specialisation. Those responsible for recruiting supervisors for a project activity have, in the past, had difficulty in finding supervisors for projects not related to the research work of faculty members.

9 Difficulty has occasionally been experienced in projects requiring industrial collaboration. It is, perhaps, inevitable that busy people, with preoccupations other than the education of students, will have different views from those of students about what should be done in a particular case. If organisations are to be involved in projects concerned with the humane application of knowledge, whose primary objectives do not include education, considerable diplomacy will have to be invoked in the give and take relationship to ensure that neither party to the arrangement indulges in all take and no give.

10 Some faculty members have questioned whether all students are ready for project work in the third year of an undergraduate course – particularly where time is likely to be wasted with false starts or where a large amount of factual knowledge is expected of graduates. Whatever one's views about teaching methods, or one's views about the value of large quantities of factual knowledge, this reaction must be anticipated.

11 In complex projects, particularly those involving groups of students, it is frequently difficult to strike a suitable balance in supervision between over-directing students' activity (which takes away initiative) and letting them have their head (which may lead to chaos).

12 With projects where several students are engaged upon a common problem, there is the question of control – where students have the opportunity to use one another's calculations, without supervision. Where it is necessary to produce a grade reflecting each individual student's ability, this can be a severe problem, though it rarely is.

13 Although there may be no objection to projects taken singly, the cumulative effect of several projects on the balance of studies in a course needs to be watched. The transferable abilities and skills stimulated by project work are not the only things expected of a graduate; some knowledge is expected too.

14 'Housekeeping' problems can also arise with project work. For example, in one department, where projects are scheduled to run for a given number of weeks from Monday to Friday, there has been a security problem concerning access to drawing boards and library from 9 a.m. to midnight.

Some of the above difficulties are fundamental academic ones; some are detailed administrative ones. Although the administrative difficulties may seem trivial by comparison with the academic ones, they may prove formidable obstacles to effective working.

THE PRINCIPAL BENEFITS TO STUDENTS ACCRUING FROM TRADITIONAL PROJECT WORK

Interestingly, some of the features which offer problems in project work also provide challenge and are occasionally mentioned by faculty as benefits. Projects concerned with the humane application of knowledge in community service should, hopefully, benefit people other than students. All projects should benefit students in at least some of the following ways which have been noted from traditional project work.

1 Much is gained from the opportunity to look deeply into a specific field of knowledge, whatever that field may be.

2 Students can gain confidence from facing a real problem, on their own, where the results are unknown and where they have to gather all their knowledge together and apply it to a real task.

3 In projects, students gain the experience of breaking down a complex task into bits suitable for study. The most difficult part of any investigation is formulating the right questions; where subjects are taught by lectures and examined by three-hour exams with short questions, there is a singular danger that students will never get the experience of formulating questions for themselves. Good projects get round this problem.

4 Some students do not perform satisfactorily when changing rapidly from one subject to the other in successive lectures, tutorials and laboratory periods. With relatively long periods of uninterrupted work, much can be achieved in projects.

5 Projects give students experience in planning time (often working against the clock) and planning their use of facilities.

6 The most frequently referred to benefit of project work is the effect on student morale. In particular, projects have been found to have high interest for research-oriented students, often revealing interests which may determine the choice of a career. Other students, too, have responded favourably to the challenge of having a problem of their own to solve.

7 In any precise, quantitative study, there is a danger of students believing that there is a single 'right' answer to any question. Projects give students personal experience of multi-solution problems.

8 Some engineering projects are effective in showing engineering in its social context; the group projects discussed below are specifically designed to do this. Other (design and make) projects give students an appreciation of the difficulties of the production process.

9 An important benefit of projects has been that of making discussion of work possible between students and supervisors. Lectures, and indeed research papers, can be 'untrue' to their subjects by suggesting that inquiry proceeds along clear, orderly routes. The experience of systematic muddle and significant chaos can show more about a person's intellectual approach than a dozen lectures, mulled over in suburban weekends.

10 Faculty members have been found to be much more interested in supervising projects of their own creation than in supervising standard classical experiments.

11 Students gain unique experience in the presentation of technical information in the form of a bound thesis, a verbal report, a document designed for the non-specialist, etc. The report on the set laboratory experiment can be a little demoralising when the student knows that the reader of his report (his supervisor) has read similar reports many times and already knows what he is likely to say; many projects give the opportunity for an individual approach and for experience of a genuine reporting situation.

THE NECESSARILY INTERDISCIPLINARY NATURE OF
PROJECTS IN THE HUMANE APPLICATION OF
KNOWLEDGE

It has been argued that disciplines are social, not intellectual, phenomena. That is to say, knowledge in a discipline is organised not through unique paradigms but rather through social institutions in which the knowledge is gathered and disseminated. In the Imperial College setting, for example, interdisciplinary could be interpreted as inter-departmental. The paradigms, methods of investigation, criteria of validity and reliability, even the specific facts, do not vary substantially between different branches of science or within engineering. There are, however, major differences of emphasis between groups of subjects. In pure science, for example, a phenomenon may be judged by the economy of hypothesis with which it may be described, the elegance with which it fits the theory; in engineering, the same phenomenon might be judged by whether it could be used in a specific system to achieve a desired effect.

If the skills to be derived from university study are to be transferable, there is clearly a place for project work or other activity which gives a student experience of a scientific or technological discipline other than his own. If properly handled, such experience should indicate to the student the way in which concepts and intellectual methods from one discipline can be used to handle information traditionally thought to belong to another. A peripheral, but crucial, benefit is that such study should give the student the chance to stand back from the particulars of his discipline and to see how problems in his major discipline are chosen, how knowledge is organised, how its reliability is tested, etc. His major discipline, and the diverse studies which it embraces, may be expected to give a student some understanding of considerations internal to the discipline. But, ultimately, it will be criteria external to the discipline which will determine its survival – value. These criteria may include efficiency, economy, utility, the social effects of specific activity, and the political consequences. The evaluation of an idea, system, device, etc. by these criteria is included among the objectives of some types of project work currently undertaken in engineering courses – but exceptionally rather than typically.

Indeed, the establishing of valid and reliable criteria of this sort is often the concern of other 'disciplines' or subjects – such as economics, ergonomics, sociology, etc. The 'ultimate' value of the criteria to individuals or societies is often the preoccupation of disciplines in the humanities – history, philosophy, etc. Recognition of this fact has often led to the associating with engineering courses of ancillary or complementary studies in the humanities and social sciences. For administrative convenience, these courses are usually taught separately from, and in parallel to, the major courses in engineering. Despite the well-meaning efforts of the staff concerned, the links between subjects which students are expected to make are frequently not made and there is a grave danger of such studies being regarded at best as a pleasant and acceptable extra, or at worst as a distracting triviality.

The value of interdisciplinary project work is that it throws emphasis on the criteria by which a student's professional knowledge is considered outside the social institutions through which his subject is defined and legitimated. If this can be done within the confines of the university, how much better if students are thrown into real situations.

THE HUMANE APPLICATION OF KNOWLEDGE FOR COMMUNITY SERVICE IN ENGINEERING PROJECT WORK

The crucial difference between the humane application of knowledge and any other application of knowledge is that the effectiveness of the enterprise is judged by the extent to which those applying knowledge have deepened their understanding of human problems and the extent to which those on whose behalf knowledge is applied have benefited. Effectiveness in this sense is extremely hard to measure. But it is recognisably different from effectiveness measured by purely economic criteria, by judgements of elegance of solution, by considerations of the extent to which knowledge represents a contribution to a discipline, etc. It follows that the most important single task, in activities linking curriculum and service through the humane application of knowledge, is that of ensuring an adequate mechanism of feed-back, of checking actual performance against intentions. Such a system must be valid not only in terms of a university's internal requirements – concerned, for example, with student assessment – but also in terms of human needs. In some work which meets the university's requirements, this last element is lacking.

For example, the scheme of group projects run by the department of electrical engineering at Imperial College has, for many years, included projects designed to give students an understanding of some of the social, political and economic aspects of their work. Project supervisors can give general indications of the suitable lines of inquiry; but in carrying out the project, it is up to the students to discover which external factors govern the application of engineering knowledge in a particular instance, and to learn by informal processes of consultation whether the solutions they provide to the problems they study are suitable ones. Typical projects involving this sort of decision are the following:

1   How far should air-traffic control over Europe be automated?
2   Examine the possibility and desirability of charging road users to keep traffic out of dense areas.
3   Investigate the possibility of associating a district heating scheme with a modern power generating plant (either conventional or nuclear).
4   Recommend methods and machinery for profitably collecting, sorting and salvaging domestic rubbish from the London area.
5   What would be the effect on the electricity supply industry of the discovery of gas in the North Sea?
6   Is the Concorde worthwhile?
7   Suggest a communications system for Pakistan whereby continual communication may be maintained throughout the country. Factors to be considered should include geography, cost, security.
8   Recommend a suitable transport system for use between central London and Foulness.
9   How should the problem of 'motorway madness' be solved?

These projects have considerable value in giving students an understanding of social questions. They also give them the experience of working as a group, of collecting and disseminating technical information from a variety of sources, etc. Indeed, the skills required for the successful carrying out of this sort of project are generalised skills which can readily be transferred to other types of work. For example, they include skill in comprehending complex documents and interpreting and extrapolating from the information in them; skill in applying different types of knowledge in practical instances; skill in analysing problems, breaking them down into their constituent parts, distinguishing fact from hypothesis, cause from effect; skill in synthesising ideas and information gathered from a variety of sources, by different people, into a unique report; skill in evaluating particular ideas, methods, systems not only in terms of such internal evidence as logical accuracy and consistency, but also in terms of such external criteria as efficiency, economy, utility, likely social effects, and possible political consequences.

All this being said, there is still the singular difficulty that, without adequate feed-back from real-life clients, there is no way of staff or students (or indeed those for whom the information they gather might be useful) knowing whether the task has been adequately carried out. Judgements about student performance have, of necessity, to be limited to considerations of whether students have carried out, in the time available, more or less than what might reasonably have been expected of them – not whether they have acquired some useful knowledge.

The group project scheme has been extended in past years to involve students in visits to developing countries, to gather information for project work at the same time as doing some useful practical work in the areas visited (see Goodlad, 1970,[5] and Brown and Goodlad, 1971[3]). Once again, there has been the problem not only of assessing the students' work by academic standards, but also of knowing whether their activity was the best way of achieving the social objectives. One group of students, for example, studied aspects of electricity supply to rural areas of Zambia and undertook some practical installation work and load surveying. Another group studied the development of Venezuela's telephone network, working on rural routes to earn their keep. A third group designed, constructed and field-tested in Tunisia a robust tape-player, for use in fundamental education schemes in tropical and semi-tropical developing countries. In each case, students carried out work of direct social utility in the context of development. However, although the students undoubtedly learned much of value in the short-term (and hopefully for the long-term too), the sheer distances involved and the impossibility of detailed academic supervision make one cautious in ascribing any dramatic social value to the work.

The possibility of meeting both academic and genuine social objectives is greater for home-based projects. There are many social problems to which engineers can usefully turn their attention. For example, the provision of heat, food, telephones and other amenities to old people is a pressing social need. The principal difficulty is that of establishing an effective contact between an engineering department and a social agency. The most satisfactory situation is when a social agency approaches an engineering department with a genuine problem to be examined.

K

As a result of an initiative of this kind, a group of Imperial College electrical engineering undergraduates studied methods of delivering hot food to old people in Hackney, during the academic year 1972–3. In 1971–2, the borough of Hackney supplied over 380,000 hot meals to old people who were either housebound or who could walk to their nearest club for a subsidised meal. Some of the food had to meet special dietary requirements, for medical or religious reasons; some was specially prepared for physically or mentally handicapped people. On an average day in Hackney, some 1,500 meals are distributed. The deliveries, which start at 11.30 a.m., have to reach any dwelling in the borough. Great attention is given to ensuring that the meals arrive regularly, for regular visits can be the focal point in the daily routine of old people who are socially isolated.

The meals are delivered in modified Ford Anglias and Dafs, by drivers and helpers. The vans carry batteries to heat portable hot-boxes which are used to transport the food. (For reasons of hygiene the food must be kept at a required temperature throughout its journey.) The portable hot-boxes are pre-heated on mains supply for one and a half hours, in the kitchens of the borough catering department. The cooked food, sealed in aluminium containers, is placed in the hot-boxes; these are placed in the vans by a turntable mechanism which allows rapid access in the delivery. Each van carries fifty meals.

The students' project was to examine the system for delivering hot food and see if it could be improved. Some of the problems were: how to keep food hot when a helper climbs four floors, to deliver food in a block of flats with no lift; how to package food so that the package can be easily delivered, but has a lid which does not cut the hands of the kitchen staff (which aluminium foil tends to do) and is easily opened by a ninety-year-old woman with arthritis; how to design hot-boxes with optimum power supply, temperature control, insulation, weight, accessibility, etc.; how to achieve the optimal routing of vehicles – taking account of parking restrictions, engine-performance characteristics, difficulty of access to each dwelling on a route, etc.

Six students were given a completely free hand to examine the existing system and report on it, with suggestions for improvements. They considered radical solutions – such as that the best way to provide hot food for old people would be for their neighbours to cook it, or that – if the visits of the helpers were more valued than the food – it might be better to distribute the heat and the food separately (supplying small ovens to the old people and distributing blast-frozen food in an unhurried routine which would facilitate greater social contact). However, a conventional meals-on-wheels system is littered with interesting technical problems through the solution of which students can acquire considerable technical knowledge. For example, students were able to study the routing of vehicles with a computer – learning a new computer language in order to do so.

The Hackney project was set up principally because the catering manager knew, through his son, who was formerly a student at Imperial College, of the sort of projects carried out by undergraduate engineers. He was, therefore, able to suggest the participation of the students in the study, in the knowledge that it would be feasible for them to take part.

Immediate solution to community technical problems apart, the least such a project achieves is a deepening of the awareness of engineering students of how and where their skills can be applied in community service, and a further spreading of knowledge about what goes on in universities.

In engineering education, the principle of having sandwich courses is already well-tried. In theory, the arrangement whereby a student spends part of his time in industrial employment and part in university study should ensure that the student's knowledge is applied in commercial and industrial situations and that his theoretical studies are informed by detailed knowledge of real-life work. Even if a sandwich scheme becomes simply a form of high-level apprenticeship, there is a possibility that some learning will take place by osmosis.

In discussing ways in which overseas project work could be improved (Brown and Goodlad, 1971[3]), we have suggested a modification of the traditional, thick sandwich course in which a student would characteristically spend a year in industry, three years at college and finally a further year in industry. The modification would involve a student in a year overseas in the *middle* of his studies. The arrangement might work as follows: a year in industry before going to college, to learn detailed practical skills such as the maintenance of diesel generators. Two years at college, carrying out the first two years of the university course, which might well include some social studies concerned with social and economic problems of developing countries, and with a first university long vacation spent in further study in industry. Then there would follow fifteen months overseas, carrying out practical work in a developing country and gathering information which could be used in a design and make project, in an individual technical project, in a dissertation, or in a group project with the general objective of applying engineering knowledge to some specific problem arising out of a human situation. Finally, there would be the third year of university study in which ideas gained in the year overseas could be written up and any necessary project work could be completed. The considerable expense of sending a student overseas would, in this way, be spread and he might be expected to carry out some work of genuine service to his hosts in fifteen months – whereas the usual three months of a long vacation is barely adequate. Needless to say, there are a host of knotty problems still to be considered – such as the difficulty of arranging a placement sufficiently far ahead for a student's social studies to inform him about economic and social conditions in the country to be visited, and the even more difficult task of ensuring that the student's field work overseas fitted in harmoniously with local needs, employment patterns, etc.

The principle of a year's placement in the middle of under-graduate studies could, however, without difficulty be applied at home. So that the project on the Hackney Borough meals-on-wheels service could be based on detailed observation of the existing scheme, a student spent his long vacation in a part-time clerical post in the catering department. Not only was he able to carry out some necessary work for the department, but he was also able to make detailed observations of all aspects of the meals service. An extension of the idea would be for a student to undertake a year's placement in a service capacity – working, perhaps, at a humble level and on mundane work not only to 'get the feel' of the grass-roots situation, but also to gather information which would be translated into design criteria or into formulation of a project for work on return to college. There is no reason at all why students should not do this sort of thing in a spirit of self-sacrificial altruism; it would be even better if the engineering institutions recognised this type of work as a valid form of training, involving responsibility relevant to the requirements for recognition as a chartered engineer. A subsidiary benefit would be the opportunity for a student to consider at leisure the direction in which he finally wished to go in his life's work, and to digest in the year away from college the often daunting quantity of detailed theoretical and factual knowledge which university courses nowadays contain.

This sort of detailed experience of grassroots situations might be expected to produce suggestions from students of suitable design and make projects and of individual technical projects. Certainly, it might be expected to suggest subjects for the sort of projects which would seem to fit most readily into existing university courses – interdisciplinary projects taking the form of problem-oriented studies, with emphasis on the evaluation and interpretation of information, rather than on experimental work. Experimental work depends upon detailed procedures learned in the context of a discipline, whereas literature searching is a technique basic to all subjects. Clearly, it would be of singular benefit if detailed experimental work could follow from such experience. Indeed, it is highly probable that the construction of a device or the specification of a system might be an appropriate follow up to the collection of data from field work. But with the outcome of such project work being thought of in the first instance as a dissertation or usable report, (possibly with associated viva voce examination), considerable flexibility of administration would be possible, as well as freedom of choice for students and supervisors.

One of the things which institutions of higher education are good at is the handling of information and the independent appraisal of activities reflecting different social perspectives. If it be accepted that to be academically respectable, knowledge need not be new to the profession, but merely new to *students*, and that its newness in specific situations is important, the possibilities are enormous. Even experience to date suggests that commercial and government organisations might value the independent study of students, who would evaluate an activity by standards not necessarily regarded as primary in terms of traditional evaluation – in fact, criteria concerned with the humane application of knowledge.

REFERENCES

1 P. H. G. Allen, 'Engineering projects for engineering undergraduates', Proceedings Conference on Innovation and Experiments in University Teaching Methods, University of London, Institute of Education, April 1968, pp 81–7.
2 P. H. G. Allen, 'Stimulating mechanical interest among students taking

electronic engineering options', Proceedings Conference on the Mechanical Aspects of Electronic Design, Budapest, April 1972, pp 469–78.
3   J. Brown and J. S. R. Goodlad, 'Grassroots Engineering', *Electronics and Power*, February 1971, pp 49–53.
4   L. R. B. Elton, 'The assessment of students – a new approach', *Universities Quarterly*, June 1968, 22.3., pp 291–301.
5   J. S. R. Goodlad, 'Project work in developing countries: A British experiment in engineering education', *International J. of Electrical Engineering Education*, 1970, 8, pp 135–40.

Chapter Seven

Fieldwork in Theological Education

BY ANTHONY DYSON

The Reverend Anthony Dyson is Principal of Ripon Hall Theological College, Oxford. He was educated at Cambridge, where he took his M.A., and at Oxford, where he took his B.D. and D.Phil. He was Select Preacher of the University of Oxford in 1970; Hensley Henson lecturer there in 1972–3; editor of the Teilhard Review 1966–72; and Chairman of the Theological Colleges Principals' Conference in 1973. Since 1969 he has been Co-Director of the Urban Ministry Project. He is author of *Existentialism*, 1965, and *Who is Jesus Christ?*, 1969, and contributor to many theological journals.

Most of the theological colleges of the Church of England were founded in the second half of the nineteenth century. With Free Church colleges and Roman Catholic seminaries, they today constitute a small and (to the outsider) curious and negligible element in the diverse world of higher education. In October 1972, the Anglican colleges contained 777 approved church candidates and 263 other students. [This category includes overseas ordinands, lay students, women's ministry candidates, ordinands of other churches, research students, etc.] Despite these modest numbers, it deserves mention that many of the colleges stand in organic relation to both older and newer universities, that some local education authorities support theological students with full or partial grants, and that the existence of the colleges is acknowledged by the National Union of Students. In fact, the theological colleges share many of the problems and possibilities, hopes and heartsearchings of the larger units in higher education and of those professional and other bodies concerned with vocational training. There is at present a deal of self-criticism, movement and experiment in the theological colleges. It is therefore worth asking whether their initiatives can be at all instructive to educators in other fields. My brief in this essay is principally to examine one experiment in one of the colleges – namely Ripon Hall in Oxford – and to consider its possible contribution to the wider scene. The project which I shall discuss is, however, only one of many and makes no claim to pre-eminence.

Before embarking upon this task, I shall first offer some general information and observations about the colleges, in order to identify features similar to, or different from, other institutions. There are at present 17 colleges, with *total* student bodies ranging from 23 to 111. They are private institutions, but have come under the effective central control of the Church through the power of the Bishops to withdraw recognition, and through oversight of fees and grants. At the present time, the usual mode of entry into the ordained ministry is by residence at a theological college after selection procedures arranged by the Advisory Council for the Church's Ministry on behalf of the Bishops. A graduate in theology does a two-year course. A graduate in a subject other than theology must spend three years in training, during which he must read for a theological degree or diploma in a university setting. A non-graduate will reside in a theological college for three years. It is not clear for how long, and on what scale, this pattern will remain the norm. The Southwark Ordination Course (with some precedents), and now the North West Ordination Course, have pioneered schemes of non-residential training. The birth of the Auxiliary Pastoral Ministry has caused a proliferation of part-time courses using resource points supplied by theological colleges, extra-mural departments, etc. Lichfield Theological College, until its recent closure, provided a form of sandwich course training which may provoke similar experiments. These varied initiatives represent not only lively and progressive thinking; they also reflect expediency and uncertainty in the face of declining numbers for the full-time ministry. It would be incautious to point to clear reasons for, or definite trends within, this flight from holy orders. This phenomenon is not of course confined to Great Britain. In general terms, it may be regarded as part of that oft-noted process of secularisation understood straightforwardly as the decline of religious beliefs and institutions. If we focus upon the theological colleges, certain more immediate factors deserve mention.

1   The number of deacons ordained annually has dropped rapidly from 636 in 1963 to 350 (estimated) in 1972. The highest number of deacons ordained in any one year in this century was in 1910. Future trends cannot be safely predicted, though the downward curve appears to be levelling out.

2 The Church of England is experiencing severe financial difficulties, whereas the cost to it of training is rising steeply (cost of grants to ordinands £283,000 in 1970, £317,000 in 1971).

3 There is uncertainty about future employment prospects in the church.

4 The growth of specialist ministries and of the number of priests in full-time secular employment creates new needs and expectations for ordinands.

5 Recent reorganisation of the colleges (entailing some closures), which was stimulated by the de Bunsen Report,[1] has provoked, but not answered, basic questions about the purposes and methods of training.

6 The rapid increase in the number of married ordinands (approximately 41 per cent in 1971) has greatly modified the 'life-style' in some of the colleges.

7 The rationale of ministry and priesthood has been, and remains, a subject of intense debate. This debate is both sociological and theological in character, and has been sharpened by the challenge to adopt a more socially and politically self-conscious understanding of ministry, and by the various reactions against this challenge. Some discussion of outstanding quality has been engendered.

The debate about ministry and priesthood is crucial. It is well known that the last decade has been marked by vigorous and often provocative theological activity. For the church at large, but for the theological colleges in particular, this has meant that fundamental questions about God, Christ, man and the world, and the nature of individual and social Christian responsibility, have consequentially produced a far-ranging discussion around such questions as: 'What is the priest for?'; 'What is his role in society and in the church at large?'; 'How (if at all) does he differ from the "lay" Christian?'; 'How is he to be trained?' It is hardly surprising that the question about *role* is dominant; this is equally the case in other professions. Is the priest a liturgical leader, a social or community worker, a theological interpreter, an educator, a counsellor, an instructor in ascesis, a biblical expositor, a charismatic leader, or a manager? Or is he an extraordinary combination of all these? Is he a specialist or a generalist? There is no simple, easily available answer to these questions. It is now widely, if not altogether universally, recognised that the precise nature and functions of Christian priesthood are not dictated once-for-all either in the Bible or in the Christian tradition. To what extent, therefore, is priest-hood defined by theological and historical considerations and to what extent by prevailing cultures? And what is the relationship between the two? This kind of discussion has been given a prac-tical edge by ecumenical negotiations, which have promised much but, as yet, have produced little. [Though account should be taken of the Queen's College in Birmingham, now an ecumenical college, and of a new federation at Cambridge including Methodists.]

Not only in the church, but in many other spheres of education too, changing social expectations and conditions of life lead to a critique of institutions, to questioning of inherited structures, to reconsideration of roles and thus to a review of training procedures. In particular we must observe a sharp conflict between 'academic' and 'practical' or 'vocational' aspects of training. Such a conflict is clearly in evidence in, for example, the teaching profession. It is acute in the theological colleges also. Is the primary purpose to mould a theologically literate mind, to foster intellectual excellence, to cultivate habits of prayer and devotion, or to impart practical skills? Is the activist conception of ministry a proper antidote to rationalistic and complacent religion? Or is it a means of escape from fundamental questions into busyness? These questions have to be worked out *in ambulando* in colleges which possess varying excellence of resources, with a wide range of abilities in the student body, with a teaching body that has no clear career structure (highly qualified tutors are paid substantially less than parish priests), and with very limited capital resources for the development of living and training amenities since, for the most part, the colleges must exist solely on income from the fees of students.

In fact, certain positive guidelines emerge from this admittedly confused and (therefore) open situation. Whatever else can and must be said about the purposes of ordination training, we are obliged to assert the following:

1 Training is a process of mutual discovery by all concerned – a process which will be such as to enable subsequent discovery.
2 The phenomenon of rapid social change implies a priest or minister formed inwardly with the capacity for an informed and critical attitude towards self, faith, church and society.
3 The theological college cannot and must not provide a once-for-all training. What it undertakes must presuppose post-ordination and in-service training, formal and informal.

4 Intellectual and vocational grounding cannot be separated when a minister is involved, as he is, with certain truth-claims relating to people in their cultural, spiritual and inter-personal life. Without that rigour, activity can become fanatical or sentimental. Without that vocational grounding and social 'placing' the intellectual rigour can become arid and dogmatic.

I shall discuss later how these four assertions might be embodied in the training process. For the present, however, I want to consider certain changes or tendencies in respect of ordination training, as they relate to these issues.

If we were to look at ordination training ten or fifteen years ago, certain features attract attention. There was a considerable preoccupation with theology as an academic discipline issuing in examinations. When a theology graduate of that era was asked how he would be employed at theological college, he frequently replied, 'Doing my General Ordination Examination.' Alongside this study there was a substantial concern about cultivating certain habits of prayer and worship. And alongside both these was 'pastoralia', practical guidance about the priest's responsibilities in relation to baptism, confirmation, marriage, sickness and death, and in relation to church organisation and law. This 'pastoralia' was supported by practical work, for example, hospital visiting, taking services in local churches, missions to parishes, etc. By the mid-sixties, unease on the part of many students became vocal. The academic study came under fire from many sides; the lack of skilled practical and vocational training was criticised. The questions about role and activity became articulate, nourished no doubt by the student movement. Exactly what kind of ministry was presupposed by the style of training here criticised? It was a parish ministry in which the conduct of worship, preaching, some teaching and the administration of the principal and lesser sacraments were central. It was a ministry of personal pastoral care, of co-operation with the welfare state amid a fairly passive laity. It was the ministry of the servant-church. It was, in fact, the kind of neighbourhood Anglican ministry which has been manifest in English life for many generations. There were, of course, many counter-tendencies and many prophetic elements, within the total picture. But all in all it was a relatively secure ministry, in a supposedly secure church, in a presumably secure society.

In the intervening years in the colleges, many changes have

occurred, of which it is now possible (at least provisionally) to take stock.

1   The college syllabus is much fuller. Colleges have been under severe pressure from many quarters to add supposedly essential elements to the curriculum, for example, psychology, sociology, educational method, counselling, etc. Colleges have, of course, found that there are practical limits as to what can be thus introduced. Nor is it clear that the rationale of such introductions has been adequately explored, either on their own account, or in relation to existing parts of the curriculum.

2   There have been signs of increasing scepticism about the purpose and value of 'academic' theology. On the one hand, this may be ascribed to the desire for 'relevance' which has marked the attitude of students in relation to many disciplines. On the other hand, it may refer more particularly to the potential minister's anxiety about the apparent lack of interest, on the part of most pople, in the Christian religion and so his desire that theological study shall relate as directly as possible to practical needs of proclamation, apologetic and deeds. Truth lies on both sides in this debate. There is little doubt that theological syllabuses in universities and colleges have been in need of scrutiny and updating. This is, more or less, in process. On the other hand, Christianity depends, in the last analysis (as I have said), upon the credibility of certain truth-claims and upon the relation of these truth-claims to human life. Lack of intellectual rigour in theology can easily engender an uncritical attitude to ephemeral fashions in church and society. Thus, there is a widespread desire that what should be studied and tested is not so much the knowledge of facts, nor even the power of argumentation, but the capacity for application. This, however, assumes that we know what is to be applied.

3   There has been an increase in the attention paid to the imparting of practical and pastoral skills. This is evidenced in the increasing proportion of the colleges' budgets devoted to this area and in the appointment at some colleges of Directors of Pastoral Training. The fields of interest are legion: communications, teaching, counselling, etc. Most colleges have learnt to draw upon help (afforded with great generosity) from appropriate institutions, rather than attempt to cover these and other areas from within the college. We must obviously ask how this development relates to our theological understanding of ministry. We must ask whether such concerns can betoken a too easy escape from ambiguities of role. Nonetheless there have been clear gains. The curate who must teach in a church school will probably do so now with better training than ever before.

I have presented a very impressionistic and palpably inadequate account of the very complex and absorbing situation of the colleges. But it should supply the outsider with some understanding of, and feeling for, the work of the colleges. I shall now consider the approach to curriculum at Ripon Hall, in order then to expand in some detail the handling of fieldwork and community service.

The curriculum is divided into three concurrent courses, designated as theological, pastoral and social studies. These are pursued in parallel by each student, from the beginning of his period of training.

1 In theological studies, using the resources of university and college, the student follows a course of study which usually leads to a formal theological qualification (degree, diploma or certificate). He must satisfy the church authorities in this regard and is normally obliged to pursue a course which covers study of the Bible, Church History, Doctrine, Ethics and Worship.

2 In social studies, and under the supervision of a sociologist who is a member of the college staff, the student is introduced to the sociological perspective and follows special courses in urban sociology, community studies, government and social services.

3 In pastoral studies, and using a wide range of outside resources, the student explores strategy and organisation, ministerial role and leadership, pastoral care and counselling, teaching, preaching, etc.

In this threefold concurrent syllabus, here described in only the briefest outline, the critical question concerns the interplay of elements. On the one hand, there is a need to develop and apply intellectual rigour to a subject in its own right, so that the student actually knows what it is about, so that he develops critical and reflective faculties. On the other hand, he must *explore how a critical appreciation of the gospel* (theological studies) relates critically to *a critical appreciation of man in his contemporary environment* (social studies) and how each critically relates to (and is related by) *a critical appreciation of ministerial and churchly activity* (pastoral studies). This interplay of disciplines raises an acute methodological problem and is also a stirring challenge to syllabus construction. But it is more than these – it is a human problem too. It concerns whether we act and reflect upon our action in a whole and wholesome manner. It concerns whether our activity feeds our reflection in a fruitful way.

From 1969 to the present, our attention to these themes at Ripon Hall has been influenced by two complementary developments, namely the Urban Ministry Project (UMP) and the scheme of Pastoral Links (PL). The Urban Ministry Project, in part founded from Ripon Hall, provides programmes of urban training for clergy, teachers, social workers, etc.; and for the students at Ripon Hall. I shall confine my attention here to its work among the last category. Once during his course an ordinand spends a month in the London area on a placement. In this placement he is an observer-participant. For part of each of the four weeks, he takes part in a series of intensive seminars. These help him to assess critically the purpose and activity of the agency to which he is attached, to survey critically the environment in which that agency is set, to place local issues in wider contexts, to feel on his pulse some of the processes of urban life and to locate these empirical understandings within a theological perspective. These seminars are served by a wide range of consultants, for example, local councillors, social workers, community workers, teachers, urban clergy, members of underground organisations, etc. In the college term following this placement, the student prepares a 'proposal for ministry' in which he sketches out his survey of the placement's locality and a delineation of its critical issues, his understanding of a purpose of Christian ministry there and the kind of strategies and projects by which that ministry might be developed in relation to those critical issues. In this way he executes a pilot project prior to a full UMP programme undertaken from a parish after ordination. Two aspects of this UMP training for ordinands deserve especial attention.

1   The placement is not a parish or a church. It is normally an agency involved in broad community interests. Therefore, the whole sequence of thought and activity leading to the 'proposal for ministry' is undertaken from a professional and psychological standpoint other than that which he now enjoys as an ordinand and will enjoy as a priest.

2   The whole operation is based upon an examination of the student's experience as an observer-participant. The daily log and

weekly report forms, with group discussion and reflection, furnish the core of the enterprise. It will be clear that the weekly seminars with theological, pastoral and social themes interweave very closely with the threefold concurrent syllabus which the student pursues during his residential course at Ripon Hall.

The Pastoral Links at Ripon Hall have grown up with and alongside the UMP development and help to supplement the intensive, but designedly brief, UMP placement. The PLs, in the Oxford and North Berkshire area, fall into three categories – educational, community and parochial. They include primary and secondary schools (with school-in-community work), psychiatric patients' club, counselling centre, local grass-roots community newspaper, rural group ministry, etc. Each student spends from one to three terms on a PL so that in a three-year course he may have undertaken between four and eight assignments. Activity on the PLs is thoroughly integrated into the working week with its studies in college and university, its worship and its common life. The PLs are thus learning/ministry situations in which the student has to undertake specific responsibilities of service. He is expected to keep a log of his activity and to complete a half-termly questionnaire report-form which deals, for example, with the 'profile' of his Link, the leadership exercised there, the theological and ethical problems raised. Each week 'projects seminars' take place in the college, in which groups reflecting, or mixing, the three PL categories examine their work with a tutor and sometimes with specially invited consultants. In turn, this material provides part of the agenda for the formal element of pastoral studies on the syllabus. From the PLs, the student begins to observe the possible dimensions and directions of ministry based on careful demographic and action survey, on a real assumption of responsibility, and (hopefully) on stringent theological and social reflection. The close relationship of the PLs to the UMP syllabus and placement work will be obvious. (The relationship is strengthened by a pioneering project now in operation whereby participants on the UMP in-service course undertake some of their programme at Ripon Hall. In particular, they review and re-review at three-monthly intervals the actual projects in which they are engaged, subsequent upon their 'proposals for ministry'. In this work they are joined by Ripon Hall students whose PLs involve them in similar projects. This reciprocity between pre-service and in-service training, as yet only in its early days, promises a new and important dimension to both sets of partners.) The fact that all PLs are arranged as teams of two or more persons, to one of whom is allocated responsibilities of leadership, creates a climate of mutual instruction and co-operation and avoids reinforcement of that 'loner' mentality apparently found among the clergy.[2]

What immediate consequences flow from this combined UMP/PL experiment? Preliminary evaluation of the UMP and PL projects suggests the emergence of different attitudes to role and work among those who have been ordained than were produced under previous forms of training. Principally, a reflective attitude to ministry is fostered. This means:

1 The student is encouraged to stretch his formal theological understanding into categories which bear upon human issues and situations.
2 The inbuilt sequence of engagement–reflection–engagement–reflection helps to develop in the student a mode of 'transforming praxis'.[3]
3 The student gives personal attention and responsibility to priorities in the use of time and energy.
4 The focus upon 'purpose of ministry' encourages clear and self-critical thinking.

What difficulties are encountered?

1 The development of UMP and Pastoral Links, with a chain reaction of interests and possibilities, creates severe budgetary problems.
2 The timetabling of an overall college programme combining college, university, UMP and Link interests against the daily and weekly rhythm of personal, family and prayerful life makes heavy organisational demands.
3 The diversity of commitment can put strain upon the student, not simply through bad organisation of time, but through problems of distance and travel, and clash of interests. Much more than this, however, a scheme of this kind raises important and delicate questions of policy direction. Student reaction serves as a most sensitive seismograph as to where the balance of curriculum is being lost. Notwithstanding, there is the natural reaction that a student's heavy personal commitment in one area leads to a loss of motiva-

tion in another. The 'theologically minded' student suspects engagement, however reflective it may be. The 'active' student suspects theological rigour as a myth of objective consciousness!

4 There is, furthermore, a need for continuous attention to staff training and responsibilities. On a scheme of this kind, every tutor in the college, whether or not he is directly involved in a particular area, must be able to participate intelligently and sympathetically in overall purposes and methods. For no aspect of a college programme is left untouched by these projects.

5 Overall there must be a balance and a dialectic between the student's freedom to shape and structure his UMP and Link work in accordance with personal convictions and the demands of the situation, and the requirements of course organisation and supervision where the need for detailed preparation is at a premium. This balance is inevitably precarious. For small institutions not only have the advantages of close personal relationships and the greater possibility of mutual care; they also presuppose limited and even strained resources, leading to the straitjacketing of students who have different learning needs and who might best pursue their studies in a variety of ways. There is also the danger in any residential form of vocational training, that horizons will become limited and attitudes unduly introspective.

6 But perhaps one of the major difficulties lies in the development of a capacity for theological reflection. In our work we have found few existing guidelines for this undertaking. Under present conditions, a student must approach his theology 'from below', for example, from the mastery of particular sub-disciplines such as languages, church history, philosophy of religion, biblical studies, liturgiology, ethics, etc. Presumably it is hoped that, gaining a mastery over tools and methods, he will emerge with the capacity for a reflection which relates to broad themes of God and man and which is discursive and critical in character. This is, however, a difficult path to travel. There tends, all too often, to be a serious gap between the intellectual and factual mastery of sub-disciplines on the one hand, and the mastery of a mode of overall reflection on the other hand. It is, of course, quite clear that this latter mastery cannot be achieved without real grasp of tools, methods and content. But there is urgent need for radical and imaginative approaches to theological and other areas of learning which will support that mode of reflection which moves between the Scylla of verbalism and the Charybdis of activism.

L

Which features of the projects described above may deserve generalisation?

1 In any form of vocational or professional training we need to consider most carefully to what extent 'theoretical' and 'practical' work should be handled in sequence or concurrently. In my judgement, the case for concurrent work is proven. Only in this way are the respective assumptions truly and radically challenged. Consideration must also be given to the comparative weighting of concurrent elements so that one element does not create over-dominant assumptions. It is not enough to offer, for example, modest lateral enrichment of a humanistic kind to a degree course in science. In practice, the 'system' of the discipline under full-time study will go virtually unchallenged.

2 I argue that *any* kind of extended learning process in a particular area should involve for the participant carefully planned and simultaneous exposure, both conceptually and practically, to a broader social setting. At present, many of the professions are marked by a strong and insular resistance to change. Where there is openness, the change has to be engendered from within the thinking and practices of the profession. I should suppose that the kind of social exposure entailed in UMP – from a professional standpoint different from that of the participant – would be even more important for a prospective teacher than the present form of teaching practice. How else do we foster in the individual educator an attitude both sensitive and critical to social change?

3 It is important in any learning process, in the arts and the sciences as well as in vocational and professional training, that the student is afforded the opportunity to consider the intellectual and social assumptions within his study and thus to relate that study to prevailing world-views and to his own emerging world-view. It is one thing to reject sectarian indoctrination of any kind; it is another thing to shelve responsibility for the formation of world-views in a plural society. In fact this is impossible since no study is value-free. It matters, therefore, that these values are exposed and examined. A theological college, developing a broad theological perspective in relation to often very practical and immediate problems, may itself therefore serve as an educational model. I do not commend a narrowly theological schema, but rather a way of reflecting upon meaning of life, social goals, cosmology and world-view, etc. I am, thus, arguing for a broad context to the learning process, a context which may well have to include (but not be exhausted by) religious and ideological features – be the institution and the course of study ever so secular; or *because* they are so secular.

4 Community service of whatever kind may not usefully be regarded as a hobby. For it determines in part, and for good or ill, the future shape of society. It also affects for good or ill the consciousness of those who engage in it. In consequence, it ought not to be undertaken unadvisedly, lightly or wantonly. It seems important that all tertiary education (and of course what precedes it) should take seriously the social dimension of responsibility which inheres in all intellectual disciplines and forms of vocational training. The aim is that, in the arts and the sciences, and in the specialised training for the professions, each person should, integrally in that undertaking, 'focus upon the implications and demands of the human situation in an open and hopeful manner'.[4] This statement has a markedly theological character – but strikes a strongly humanistic note too. Its relevance extends far beyond the clergy and their training, though for them it points, in fact, to the outlines of a role which is both theologically articulate and humanly grounded.

REFERENCES

1 *Theological Colleges for Tomorrow*, CIO, London, 1968.
2 See L. Paul, *The Deployment and Payment of the Clergy*, CIO, London, 1964, pp 81–2.
3 See Paulo Freire, *Pedagogy of the Oppressed*, Penguin, Harmondsworth, 1972, pp 60–1.
4 D. Jenkins in, *Technology and Social Justice*, ed R. H. Preston, SCM, London, 1971, p 223.

Chapter Eight

A Sandwich Course in Sociology

BY NANCY BURTON AND STEPHEN COTGROVE

Nancy Burton is Senior Lecturer and Director of Social Work Studies in the School of Humanities and Social Sciences, University of Bath. She has been closely involved with the establishment and development of the sandwich element in the Sociology course at Bath. For over thirty years, she has been involved in teaching in schools, the services, penal and corrective establishments, and various institutions of further and higher education. She is also a magistrate.

Stephen Cotgrove has been Professor of Sociology at the University of Bath since 1966. He is a member of the Council for National Academic Awards and a member of the Schools Council. Among his principal writings are *Technical Education and Social Change*, 1958, *The Science of Society*, 1967, *Science, Industry, and Society*, (with S. Box), 1970, and *The Nylon Spinners*, (with J. Dunham and C. Vamplew), 1971.

Some reflections on the first nine years of the sandwich course in sociology at Bath:

The four-year sandwich course in sociology at Bath took in its first twenty-four students in 1963. The annual intake has now doubled and the number and ('A' level) quality of applications suggests that this kind of course is very attractive to a certain type of student, mainly female, with an instrumental rather than an intellectual approach to the experience of higher education. The nature of the course pre-selects the applicants and this constraint must, to some extent, affect other aspects of the course, including recruitment, activities, and interests of staff as well as of students.

AIMS

The course was designed as a vocational course, in the Bristol College of Science and Technology, out of which the University of Bath developed. The intention was to explore the possibilities of applying the sandwich method, well established in engineering, medicine and nursing, teaching and social work, to the teaching of the social sciences. This article will be concerned mainly with the experience of the sociology course, but an economics and administration course ran concurrently as a sandwich course and is still running. Many of the conclusions drawn from the experience of the sociology placements, apply equally validly to the economics course.

Athough the sociology course provided fourth-year options leading to recognised qualifications in teaching, personnel management and social work, it aimed primarily to provide a training in the application of sociological skills and methods. While it was not too difficult to organise a placement system for those students committed to one of the three professionally qualifying options, the real innovation lay in trying to adapt the mixed practical/theoretical techniques of training in applied science, to the study and practice of social science. It is this problem that all social science sandwich courses have been exploring, since their rapid expansion in the 1960s. To stress the strictly vocational content of a sociology course is to avoid the issue: the rationale for practical work in industry, teaching, social work, is obvious for students aiming to work in those fields. But where does the student who wants to spend four years studying sociology, fit into a placement pattern?

Sociology is both a theoretical study of conceptual systems and an attempt to develop scientific methods of measurement and analysis to problems of social engineering. There is a knowledge component and a technique component in sociological studies. Students of the subject, therefore, can use their placement experience to practise techniques of social engineering and they can (using the enlightenment model of Janowitz (1971)) use their sociological knowledge to interpret their placement experience, and their placement experience to validate or challenge the theoretical teaching provided in the academic content of the course.

Sociology can provide models for the organisation and interpretation of experience. It combines an intellectual training in the handling of abstract concepts with a training in the use of quantitative methods of measurement and evaluations of social data. It was on this basis that the Bath sociology sandwich course was organised. All students, whether with firm vocational interests or none, are encouraged to see the placement as one primarily related to sociology, rather than to business management, social administration, teaching or any other vocational goal. The degree to which this is successful depends on the integration of practical and academic work throughout the course. But the attempt to achieve this for all students is crucial. A well-integrated placement experience can demonstrate to a student of a theoretical discipline that higher education is essentially an exposure to a supervised learning experience, undertaken both intra-murally, within the university, and extra-murally, in the world of employment and work. A four-year process of interpretation of the world of affairs by the world of academia and vice versa, has many potential benefits for both. Not least, it takes the student into the world.

ORGANISATION

A placement system based on these assumptions must be planned as systematically as the academic programme. It must be planned in conjunction with the academic programme and by members of the academic staff who are involved in teaching. A haphazard system of placements found by students for themselves without reference to the academic staff or the relevance of the placement to the students' interests and studies is wasteful of a potentially valuable learning situation. The integration of academic and practical work requires that the placement shall be seen, not as an unrelated episode in the student's life, but as an experience to be interpreted and absorbed throughout his university career.

This means that, ideally, the academic staff must participate actively in seeking placements, in discussing them with students, prospectively and retrospectively, and must keep in touch with the student during placement, at least minimally. All this is time consuming; for the staff it means devoting to students on placement time that might otherwise be used on research, leading to publications and possible academic preferment. No academic credit will accrue to the staff for successful placement preparation and supervision. No allocation of timetable hours may be made for this part of his work. At managerial levels, even in universities committed to the sandwich method, there are no very senior appointments specifically earmarked for staff involved in placements. Indeed, it is frequently suggested that placements could be equally well organised by the administrative staff of the faculty or school, as if in fact the arrangements were primely administrative. At Bath, some schools do use their administrative officers for this purpose. In the school of humanities and social sciences we have resisted this, emphasising the essentially academic function of introducing the student and the course to the placement agency and supervising the contact throughout the placement.

It may well be asked: where are the social sciences sociology staff with the wide range of practical contacts necessary to find placements for sociology students? Academic appointments are based on academic achievement and promise rather than on practical contacts. An active placement programme requires staff to be aware of potential and actual developments in applied sociology, but academic promotion will go rather to staff aware of the latest academic publications. Perhaps there is a case for the establishment of an appointment in academic institutions concerned with the development of sandwich courses, that shall be primarily concerned with developing this form of learning opportunity, on the analogy of a visual aids lecturer or an information officer.

Apart from staffing, the sandwich course itself needs careful timetabling; at Bath we rejected the thick sandwich in favour of the thin sandwich. We felt that for a student to be away from university for one year in four was to cut him off from academic work too drastically. We prefer to sandwich the six months practical between solid wedges of academic work, so that there can be time for the digestion and interpretation of the practical work. We see this six months in placement primarily as a learning rather than an earning experience. In a six months practical the student can still maintain his status *as a student*, in his own eyes and those of the agency within which he is working. He is not a temporary employee: in fact he can remain on student grant for a large part of the placement, in appropriate situations. As a student on placement, he may enjoy the security and independence of a student simultaneously with the responsibility of an employed person.

Let us assume that the practical applications of the social and behavioural sciences (economics, psychology, politics and sociology) are accepted. What types of practical work are then seen as relevant? There is a strong temptation to follow the tradition established by the well established sandwich courses in social work teaching, medicine and nursing, and to place students for a trial period in the kind of setting they will be working in when they graduate and qualify. Thus, students work in social work settings; in schools of all kinds; in industry. They observe how the systems operate and participate in operating them. We have not adequately explored the opportunities for students to observe 'the other side', to experience the reception of social welfare, medical care, or education, to work in a placement as a client rather than as an administrator of the system. True, we have placed students in community work placements, in welfare rights movements, in shop floor jobs, and with down and out vagrants, alcoholics and other social problem groups. On the whole, though, we accept the conventional definitions of social problems and set our students to work in the conventional settings organised to contain and deal with them. For those students who reject the paternalism of the welfare state, there are the protest and pressure groups on behalf of the disadvantaged and deprived, and there are activities (for example, adventure playgrounds) which are sufficiently unorthodox to attract the anti-establishment student.

We have found that a wide range of students will find some placement of this type interesting. By no means all students going on placement in, for example, the police, social service or general welfare setting, will have a vocational interest in working after graduation in these areas. They will see the placement as an exposure to a social system in miniature, providing material with which to explore ideas of deviance, organisation theory, social relationships, social change, etc. which they have encountered in their academic work.

Some students each year are placed in research agencies. We have tried hard to persuade local authorities to regard these as grant-earning placements, in order that we can place a student in a research unit able to offer him valid useful experience. It is not our intention that students should work for six months as cheap, intelligent clerical labour, and call this 'research experience'. If the student has to find a *job* in research he has not much choice of agency or project. If he is looking for an opportunity to undertake supervised work, or better still, to plan and help carry out a discrete stage of a project, or undertake one of his own, as a student on a grant, this may provide a really useful experience. He will learn what happens under the name of research, whether he wants to work in research after graduation and how far the teaching he has received on research methods is applied or applicable. In essence, the placement must be seen as another form of observing and understanding systems, techniques and relationships, within any given institutional structure. It is essentially the function of staff on a sandwich course to help the student to do this.

If a student is anxious to pursue an individual project in his placement period, he may do this, under staff supervision. He may spend the period designing and following up his own inquiry into some area that interests him, or attach himself to a member of staff who needs a research assistant for a short period for a specific job to be completed. The one unyielding principle of placements should be that the student sees some interest and relevance in his programme.

COSTS AND BENEFITS

What are the drawbacks to this system? Not all students are, by personality, fitted to this type of experience. The ambiguous status of the student/trainee/employee in the placement situation is intolerable to some and, if it coincides with a period of intense personal stress, can lead to breakdown and withdrawal. Students who are alienated and isolated in the academic setting will find their problems increased. Panic, aggression, withdrawal and depression may manifest themselves as a result of role strain and loneliness. Students will need help and support over these crises from academic staff and, if possible, from supervisors. Though such experiences can be seen, with the help of a sympathetic and wise teacher, as a confrontation with reality, in which the student learns about himself and his fantasies, some students simply cannot tolerate them.

Apart from such painful experiences of maturation through adversity, what are the significant benefits to students of the sandwich course? These may be considered as falling under two headings, (1) personal and social, and (2) academic.

For many students, coming to university straight from school, it is a maturing experience. They have had to develop qualities of tact, and perception strategies of management of situation, which would not have been called into existence in the university world.

Further, many students can see this as a job rehearsal experience, which enables them to make an informed choice of career after graduation. The actual placement experience may lead to a student being offered a job on graduation, or being short listed in a competitive field because of the relevance of his placement. A student with placement experience may have an advantage of six to twelve months' experience over a non-sandwich course student, in applications for first jobs. Whether this advantage is retained over the first few years in a job or not, it is a significant bonus at the period of job-seeking in the last year of a course. Contacts are made on placement which may lead to opportunities of post-graduate work. Interests, started in the lecture and seminar room, in medical care systems, criminology, urban growth, child development, social policy, housing, have been nurtured by placements and have blossomed into postgraduate studies and research, or into employment in those fields. Students' academic interest has been focused, their motivations reinforced. This is reflected in active, lively and critical response to academic teaching. The class can become a dialogue between teacher and student, where the student may contribute a monitoring and realistic comment based on his experience. Theoretical studies can be shown to be related to social situations and relationships encountered by the student.

Bath sociology students have travelled on placement to and in the following countries: Afghanistan, Australia, Canada, Denmark, France, Holland, India, Israel, Mauritius, South America, Sweden, Turkey and the USA. They worked in blind welfare, child welfare, counselling, correctional and educational establishments; they explored the education of Welsh children in Patagonia, the land gift movement in India, the culture of poverty in Mauritius, the Folk High School movement in Sweden, the socio-medical services of Holland, youth provision in Newfoundland, and educational testing methods in USA. Much fourth-year academic work is based on the third-year placement, since students follow up in final-year dissertations themes and inquiries first encountered on the placement.

The third partner in this association is the placement. What benefits accrue to them from the contact with students and academics? Some gain financially: voluntary agencies now demand quite substantial fees for supervising students. But a student can be an embarrassment: no office space for him, no work load: some senior executive has accepted the student placement in principle but left it to a junior officer to organise a programme. And the student is left in an uncomfortable and ambiguous position, the focus of departmental conflict. Where a student is intelligently used to undertake a job no one else has had time or training to do, such as composing a training manual, or writing a syllabus for the teaching of sociology in sixth form general studies, the host organisation can benefit materially. Projects such as the organisation of play groups, tenants' associations, and running adventure play-grounds depend heavily on student labour. Local authority departments of social service have recruited student labour to administer surveys of the elderly and physically handicapped. Schools for gypsies, projects for the housing and employment of ex-prisoners, research into the backgrounds of homeless vagrant men – these are some of the projects in which our students have been offered work. One or two students have had their assistance acknowledged in the foreword to the publication of the results they helped to produce. Students have resources of physical, mental and emotional energy that can be highly productive if appropriately and skilfully deployed. Or they can be utterly wasted without administrative control, planning and supervision.

What part is played by staff in this situation? It has already been suggested that, ideally, staff should themselves be convinced of the significance of the sandwich pattern and play an active part in it. This means not only concerning themselves with the student on placement, but with the placement itself. It involves interpreting to the student the sociological significance of his experience. Uncounted, untimetabled hours of informal tutorial time will pass in this kind of staff–student contact. Predictably, some staff will find this pastoral, personal form of teaching distasteful. Those whose interests are subject rather than student oriented will avoid or reject it.

The Bath course has never satisfactorily solved the problem of assessment of placements, as an integral part of an academic course. There are too many variables – the student, the placement, the supervisor – to make a quantitative, objective assessment method possible. The evaluation of placement experience is essentially subjective. If the student measures academic progress in terms of marks or grades achieved, he may reject the placement as an inessential and peripheral experience to the winning of a good degree. The student and some academic staff may perceive time on placement as an interruption to the real task of acquiring theoretical knowledge in the traditional manner, through reading, discussing and writing. We have tried to demonstrate that, in certain carefully chosen placements, this type of student may, in a research setting, find similar or better opportunities for this kind of learning.

Finally, the students' interpretation of this type of course and experience. Most of our students would reject the term 'community service' to describe what they are doing when they participate in an adventure playground, a housing advice centre, schools for autistic, deprived, maladjusted delinquent or handicapped children etc. This opportunity presents them with a chance to learn about the organisation, its problems, clients, personnel and values and incidentally to learn about themselves and the society in which they have grown up. Placements are selected by students because the work appears to be interesting, that is, relevant to their interests, rather than because it offers opportunities for 'service'. Students are attracted to involvement in an activity which they can see to be socially useful and directed towards the benefit of deprived and disadvantaged. But they do not see themselves as do-gooders.

THE FUTURE

Both our experience at Bath, and the evidence of wider researches, indicates the very real potential of sandwich courses over a wide range of subjects. It has probably always been true that only a minority of students are highly intellectually involved in university life. And the development of courses with a consciously vocational orientation meets a real need. But we would wish to stress that it is their value as an educative experience which is the real justification for sandwich courses.

To draw rigid distinctions between knowledge and experience, learning and doing, is in any case false. Both intellectual study and future career are activities of the self in which the individual is discovering, developing and expressing a self or identity. We need to see the tertiary stage of education as part of an extended transition between childhood and adult roles. The medical student is not only learning medicine: he is *becoming* a doctor. To postpone until after graduation any thoughts as to what one will 'be' is, for most, unrealistic. And the strength, as well as the challenge, of sandwich courses is in the opportunity which they provide for an integrated educative experience, in which the student learns a subject, explores its relevance to the world of affairs, brings questions from the 'real' world back into the lecture room, learns more about himself by trying future adult roles for 'fit', and in the process has the chance to develop his own identity.

What is difficult is to challenge the entrenched view that such courses are not for the intellectual high fliers. The problems of the real world are no easier to solve than are those of academia. Indeed, the challenge and opportunities for intellectual development are certainly as great as in the more traditional courses. Those of our students who are 'academics' and have gone on to postgraduate study have been just as enthusiastic about the placement experience, with its opportunity to learn at first hand some of the problems of research design, conceptual clarification, or to expore the relevance of theoretical models to the real world which they purport to explain.

But the costs and difficulties must not be underrated. The fact that course and future career may be more closely related means that uncertainties about career are also doubts about the course. While there may be less need for an appointments officer in the traditional sense, there may be more need for earlier counselling which recognises the possible close relation between educational, vocational and personal problems.

The sheer practical problems can daunt any but the most convinced. Finding suitable placements and devoting the extra care and attention which some students will need is demanding enough. If sandwich courses were to become more popular the placement problem would become more acute. Despite lip-service to the sandwich principle, recent changes in policy have made it more difficult for students to get grants for some kinds of placements, while voluntary agencies are increasingly demanding higher training fees. And it's not going to be easy to find academic staff with the breadth of experience, ability and drive to take on the not very rewarding task. It's not the kind of job that can be left to the departmental 'dogsbody'. But if society can be convinced of the value of such courses, it will also have to face up to the costs.

REFERENCES

1 F. Musgrove *et al.*, *Sandwich Course Studies*, University of Bradford, 1970.
2 S. Cotgrove, 'Sandwich Courses: Myth and Reality', *Paedagogica Europaea*, 1973, vol 8.

Chapter Nine

Summer Projects for Children with Language Difficulties

BY ERIC HAWKINS AND JUNE DERRICK

Eric Hawkins is Director of the Language Teaching Centre at the University of York. He was formerly headmaster of Calday Grange Grammar School. He was a member of the Plowden Committee, 1963–6; member of the National Committee for Commonwealth Immigrants, 1965–8; and since 1967 has been organiser of summer schools in Huddersfield and Halifax Local Education Authorities. He is author of *Modern Languages in the Grammar School*, revised edn 1966, and of *A Time for Growing – A Handbook for Organisers of Summer Projects*, 1971.[4]

June Derrick is Senior Lecturer in the Language Teaching Centre, University of York. From 1966 to 1971 she was organiser of the Schools Council Project in English for Immigrant Children at the University of Leeds. She is author of *Teaching English to Immigrants*, 1966.

In this chapter we want to look at summer projects in which university or college students work with school children for a continuous period of several weeks during vacation time. This is a very different situation from the one described in Eric Midwinter's chapter, in which students are in sustained contact with EPA school children during term time, within the school itself or closely attached to it, and in close contact with their course tutors. It means a different kind of involvement on the part of the student: he volunteers to give up part of his vacation in order to work with the children; he may not be committed to teaching as a career, and he may not be a student of any discipline that is immediately or obviously relevant to the teaching situation he finds himself in; he will probably not be working with tutors he meets in term time, and it is likely that he has had little training specifically for the work he has undertaken in coming on the project. (More discussion of all these issues is needed, especially to see how summer project work might have a closer link with the curricular studies of at least some students and to suggest improvements in the existing modes of operation.)

There is great variety in the summer projects that have been reported in the past four or five years, but as our experience has been with language projects, mainly for non-English-speaking immigrant children and more recently for English children who are backward in reading, it is these we shall deal with here. First then, let us look at the basic thinking which brought projects like this into being. We begin with the key fact that immigrant children – who by now comprise 3·3 per cent of the total school population – live, almost without exception, in the central areas of industrial towns and cities. For all children in these areas, holiday times are not necessarily the best times of the year; for families where both parents are at work, or on the other hand where there may be unemployment and a shortage of resources, school holidays pose additional problems. For immigrant children from non-English-speaking families, there is one problem that arises in vacation and affects them in particular: with the schools closed, they are cut off from their main contact point with the English language. In term time school is the one place where they are actively taught English and obliged to use it: in their homes, in their shops, playing with friends in the areas where they live, they have little call – or opportunity – to use English. Some of what they have already learnt at school gets rusty and forgotten during the holidays. The schools stand empty and unused – except for the painters and maintenance men.

Summer language schools for immigrant children grew naturally out of this situation. Why not bring the children back into school – or into a kind of school – for a part of their holiday and provide them with teachers or companions who would go on talking English with them, chipping away at the rust, and – hopefully – developing their mastery of English in all sorts of ways that are not possible in the conventional term-time school situation? Why not do the same thing for native English-speaking children with learning difficulties, especially children backward in reading, whose problems often relate to distressing family circumstances and who, like immigrant children, seem especially likely to benefit from sustained personal contact with an adult and from some additional teaching? Summer schools, holiday projects of other kinds, especially the popular *colonies de vacances* run in France and enrichment programmes in the USA, suggested a model. The wide and varied pattern of voluntary work done by students could readily embrace this: from humble beginnings in a joint York University–Huddersfield LEA venture in 1967 have developed many and varied schemes, some of them for immigrant children, many of them multi-racial in character (Hawkins, 1971;[4] Townsend, 1971[6]).

Basically, a summer project depends on a group of student volunteers working in an area for a three to four week period, either home-based or coming in from outside and 'camping' or at least living in very economical circumstances in a local school or other building. They may be assisted by other local volunteers, especially fifth or sixth formers from the area's schools. Leadership is, of course, vital so that the volunteers' efforts are organised profitably and so that an acceptable structure is created for both volunteers and children. This may be managed through a student committee, but a director who assumes ultimate on-the-spot responsibility for the running of the project has been shown by experience to be a key figure. He is the vital link between the volunteers and the local authority and its schools, whose responsibility the children are. His is more than ever a key role, especially at a time when the aims and aspirations of the student today may apparently be running counter to those of the establishment and of the schools. The idealism and inexperience of students often make them unsympathetic to the constraints under which local education establishments have to manage their affairs. A particular difficulty of the summer projects may be the students' attempt to offer children fresh and stimulating experiences which conflict with, rather than complement, the children's experiences in school. A mode of operation has to be found that draws on the best of students' enthusiasm and strength and, at the same time, has relevance to the school's curriculum and educational aims.

It is necessary to say here that we recognise the world of difference between the linguistic and the social needs of indigenous and immigrant children. The former have the linguistic tools with which to communicate with one another, with teachers or students or visitors; what they may need is enrichment, the opportunity to use lauguage for a variety of new and stimulating purposes, to gain confidence in their own power over words, and a new self esteem which can grow out of this and out of the personal relationships that help establish it. Indeed, a stable relationship with someone in a teaching role, someone who can provide them with a great deal of uninterrupted attention, may be their prime need. Many immigrant children, on the other hand, do not have a solid enough groundwork in English for basic communication, though their social adjustment is often excellent in spite of this. More important even than an adult's reassurance and involvement in their problems may be the adult's ability to help them internalise the structures of spoken English and the vocabulary and conversational phrases that enable them to deal with everyday situations. Moreover, where the indigenous child may find it no problem to take a bus across town to a park or zoo, for the immigrant this may represent a whole range of problems. He is hedged in by ignorance often of basic local information and know-how. While all children benefit from having their environment enriched and extended, some lack the means of access even to the neighbouring suburbs.

PRACTICALITIES

The shaping of a summer project grows out of decisions relating to local needs and the availability of help and resources. The practical matters relating to these are well documented in the sources quoted at the end of this account: the recruitment of children, tutors and students, and the details of course finance have to be worked out in detail well-beforehand. Financial help from sources such as the urban renewal fund (administered by the Home Office) or the community relations commission and from local education committees is not given at short notice. Estimates have to be prepared fully twelve months ahead for the most part, and recruitment has to be well in hand by the middle of the spring term. Students make their vacation plans well in advance. Recruitment involves publicity of various kinds, posters, descriptive handouts, visits to schools to talk to sixth formers, ways and means of answering inquiries and generally helping students to understand what it is they are volunteering for.

In general, there is no fixed pattern of recruitment nor the type of student who offers his services. The individual's personality and sense of social responsibility, perhaps too his sheer curiosity about a fairly novel way of spending part of the vacation – 'three weeks in another town' – all these are more significant factors than the course of study the student is following. Or at least, this is how it has been so far. We might ask at this point whether there could not be a more closely thought-out connection between students'

M

chosen courses of study and their work on a summer project, and whether therefore there should not be a more planned recruitment, for example, especially from language or education students, and possibly from students of sociology as well. Obviously, college of education students who are training for entry to the teaching profession can bring skills and insights to the learning process which others may not have, and in turn can find a special relevance in the experience. Similarly, students of linguistics, of English or modern foreign languages, may have a special concern with language development and language learning problems. A project provides them with individual case studies that can go into considerable depth.

Whatever professionalism students bring to a project, and whatever their particular interest in the work, it is clear that for most of them they can only be as effective in working with children as the professionals allow them to be. Certainly, they are helped to be twice as effective if they are given professional guidance and support, which is why it is ideal, if not essential, to have local teaching staff working with them and the children, and why too college or university tutors can make an important contribution. Indeed, if the links with students' curricular studies are to be made explicit, then the presence of college tutors *is* essential.

How exactly teachers and tutors give help to volunteers depends on how many of them there are (and up till now there have not been many) and the type of project it is. An ideal pattern is for the volunteers to work in small teams, each team led by a trained teacher or tutor who can thus help to give a structure to the team's work, planning a day-to-day programme with the students, helping to organise the preparation of materials, and offering on-the-job guidance when students are working with the children. The more demanding the task of the students, the more desirable it is for the teams to be smaller and the support closer and more sustained. Many a volunteer effort founders on lack of this kind of support; without it, work can easily become purposeless, students and children frustrated, time wasted and tempers frayed. Goodwill on its own is not enough to sustain a meaningful day-long relationship between child and volunteer. A deeper understanding of the child's learning processes, of the cultural or linguistic problems that may arise, is something that the teacher or college tutor has to help with, and where again, for the language or education student, the personal gain can be considerable.

Where a student's aim is to build up an immigrant pupil's mastery of English, which may include his reading and writing skills, it has proved to be a great gain when there has been at least occasional contact with the teacher who has so far been responsible for teaching the child. A student may suggest a theme for himself and the child to work on, only to discover gradually that the whole of the previous term has been spent on it and the child is thoroughly bored. Although some information about the child's attainment and work may be provided beforehand, it can never be detailed enough. As students find out more about children's learning difficulties, they usually have a spate of questions they would like answered professionally. Therefore, in addition to *regular* teachers' help throughout a project, irregular help by way of teachers visiting the project weekly is something to be encouraged and planned for.

But school holidays for most teachers are a welcome and necessary break from routine, a time when they are glad to lose contact with the children they teach all term. Most city schools have more than their share of social and educational problems, and a breathing space is necessary for all concerned. Local teachers willing to return for three or four weeks of the summer holiday are not easily found. If they are, and are expected to give of their professional services, then there is a good argument for paying them a professional fee: in some areas funds have been made available for this.

Finally, in all the preliminary planning, there are the children themelves to be thought of well in advance, and – in co-operation with their teachers and parents – invited to attend the summer school. As suggested earlier, who exactly the project is intended for is a decision that has to be worked out carefully with the local education authority. It is no good aiming to run it for non-English-speaking newcomers if in fact there are few or none. If the schools have isolated a particular set of needs that they feel can be met in a project, for example, the exploration of the neighbourhood, or the improvement of children's reading skills, then these will obviously condition choices and affect recruitment. One lesson that most projects have learnt, is that information given to children far ahead of a project is easily lost or forgotten; that enrolment at the start of a project is often lower than expected; that after a few days brothers and sisters and all the neighbourhood may roll up and a firm line has to be taken about who is to be allowed in and who, if any, excluded.

Undoubtedly, one of the best forms of preparation for working on the project is for volunteers to meet the children beforehand in a variety of circumstances. Again, for many reasons, this is not always possible and a substitute is offered by way of information and training sessions beforehand. These may take place at intervals in the summer term; they are an expense, and often miss out volunteers who are busy with examinations or are simply too far away to attend the meeting (a special risk if students are recruited from many institutions to work on the same project). Additional training and information sessions are thus often held on the day or so immediately before the project.

Volunteers want to know as much as possible about the children they are going to work with, their background (particularly if it is an unfamiliar one like that of children living in a Muslim community), and their interests; they also want facts about living conditions, opportunities for recreation and time off. This kind of information is a preliminary to what one might call the real training. This needs to consist of an introduction to the discipline involved, especially language training, and to the methodology. It easily becomes all talk and too little doing, especially if students are totally unfamiliar with the subject. Short films, video tapes or tape/slide programmes can do wonders to make the teaching situation come alive and give the students the feel of the work. (Some time on each project should perhaps be given to the preparation of this type of material for future recruiting sessions.) There has to be plenty of time for questions. Ideally, there should be workshop sessions where students begin to prepare teaching materials and analyse language activities. This will possibly set them on the track of collecting and preparing apparatus (pictures, word games, puzzles, photographs and other data) well in advance of the project. (As suggested earlier, the actual requisitioning of expendable materials, books, etc. has to take place many months before the project is to begin.)

THE FEEL OF THE THING

Against this background of the educational problem in our cities and the potential contribution to be made by student volunteers in summer projects, it is time perhaps to look at one or two specific projects in more detail. An example of a 'social enrichment' project is that organised in Huddersfield in 1972. From the modest beginnings in 1967, mentioned earlier in this chapter, this project has developed under the guidance of Trevor Burgin, the educational organiser with responsibility for immigrant and remedial education, into a complex project in five different centres in the town, involving some 250 children in each centre (1,200 in all) and a total of 235 volunteers, including 130 sixth formers from Huddersfield schools. The organisers quite deliberately chose to make all the activities in the five centres 'socially orientated', concentrating on recreational pursuits rather than on language teaching, though keeping 'second-phase language help' as a subsidiary objective. The student volunteers for this project include parties from overseas. A small group of students from the University of Lund in Sweden have now taken part in three projects. The cost (£3,000 in 1972) is met by the Huddersfield LEA. Evaluation of such a project is difficult since it aims at the intangible development of personal relationships, but it is significant that the juvenile liaison department of the West Yorkshire Constabulary again noted a drop in the number of incidents involving children in this age group during the three weeks of the project.

A project we can speak about from more direct knowledge is the York-Halifax summer school, now in its fourth year. It aims quite specifically at language teaching of a fairly intensive kind, for both immigrant children and slow readers within the borough, though its objectives have only evolved over several years of experimentation. The volunteers, drawn mainly from York University and St John's College, York, are housed in a school building where the classrooms are temporarily converted into dormitories. Local sixth formers also work with the students. The school buildings in or near the immigrant area of the town are used as bases for the teaching, though additional premises can be made available as new needs arise, for example, to cater for a group of immigrant mothers who wish to learn English, or to provide a crèche for their babies. The intention is to provide one volunteer for every child, though as numbers fluctuate a student may find himself with more than one child for the day, or for the whole period of the summer school. Students work in groups, each with an experienced group leader and with a home-base in a classroom.

The pattern of the days' and weeks' activities varies, but goes something like this. The morning is timetabled so that there is an alternation of work in pairs with work in groups of about fifteen or twenty. Children arriving in the morning go first to their groups and pick up the previous day's discussion, or attempt an account of the previous evening's activities or television viewing. The student then introduces a piece of work he has planned, a language exercise, or some discussion based on a passage from a book. Out of this emerge various language points that he works on with his pupil, for example, a grammatical point, some vocabulary, or a difficult feature of English pronunciation. Usually there is a mid-morning break, after which, to vary the pattern, the group leader or one of the volunteers takes a lesson with the whole group, perhaps for songs, a story or some language games. Out of this emerge more language points, to be followed up in pair work again before the end of the morning. Some smaller groups of three or four spend the last part of the morning on a small project together, such as preparing a tape or writing and rehearsing a play to perform for the others.

Lunch can be a further opportunity for students and children to sit together and continue their talk, but in later Halifax projects this has had to be given up for reasons of expense and the children go home for lunch (they all live within five minutes of the project schools). Some projects have, in principle, decided that lunch time is a necessary break from contact with the children and provides fresh energy for the afternoon's activities. The latter tend to be less structured, often consisting of explorations of the neighbourhood in twos and threes, visits to park or museums or other places of interest. When the activities include sports or swimming, the transport arrangements and issue of equipment need careful planning. An art and craft room provides a base for individual or group activities and can play an enormously important role in the project.

Part of the late afternoon or evening is generally spent by the students discussing the day's work and in making long and short-term preparations. A group, for example, may discover that an interest in a certain topic (say animals, road safety, or pollution) is emerging and begin to plan their work around it accordingly. This calls for the planning of extra visits and arrangements, such as the hiring of a coach to the zoo, the purchasing of films for cameras, the searching for extra reference books in libraries. Above all, it means thinking out the learning potential of the children, and this is where teachers and tutors are most needed, at least to ask the right questions, though not always to answer them. For instance, what additional vocabulary will the children need to talk about the visit to the zoo? What kinds of questions can they be helped to ask? What information can they hope to seek from a zoo-keeper? What broad classifications about animals, their young, their habitat, their appearance, their foods, their noises, might they make? What language learning can take place throughout this inquiry? Will it spoil the enjoyment of the visit if the students insist on the learning?

As students get to know the children, they are able, to some extent, to predict their needs and reactions. In particular, they become familiar with the immigrant children's difficulties in learning standard English, especially features of pronunciation and grammar that almost all find equally difficult. They also need to teach new vocabulary, especially the vocabulary needed to discuss the shared experiences of the day. Resource books on the teaching of English as a second language, on pronunciation and grammar, and books containing ideas for language and other activities have to be readily available. Suitably graded reading books, books of simple science, history or geography, and reference books about the locality seem regrettably hard to come by.

For the students teaching backward readers there are, of course, a different set of problems. Often it is the talk and the building up of confidence and trust in the child, that seems more important than anything that can be labelled teaching. But exploring the bountiful stock of books supplied by the LEA remedial service, devising and constructing simple word games, and helping children to write their own books and poems become increasingly important activities with some of the children, and ones that college of education students, already trained in some measure in the teaching of initial literacy, are better able to cope with than most other volunteers.

An important feature of the Halifax project is the contact with the pupils' homes. Evening sessions are arranged when the school is open, tea made and an open invitation given to parents. Four such evenings were arranged during the three weeks of the last project. Contacts thus made were followed up by visits to the parents' homes. The parents' support is crucial in motivating the children, and undoubtedly this factor has accounted for the very high attendance figures throughout the project in the past.

EVALUATION

What then does it all add up to, both for the children and for the students? For the students especially it is worth asking this question. One can see benefits for the children, not necessarily measurable ones in terms of language test scores or improvements in reading ages, but all the same very obvious ones in terms of their enjoyment, willing participation in a variety of activities, continued attendance, affection for the students who have been their companions for three or four weeks and keenness to come on future projects. For children with learning difficulties, children very often whose difficulties relate partly to social circumstances and their lack of an adequate and productive relationship with an adult, the gains are most obvious of all. Some of the most successful work of summer projects has undoubtedly been with native English-speaking children who are backward readers.

For the volunteer there are several areas of learning: in a general sense he gets a deeper understanding of urban deprivation, of the problems of children who grow up and have their schooling in certain kinds of schools in a certain kind of area, and whose circumstances till now have been no more than the grey images of the sociology text book or the TV documentary. By this sustained involvement in the summer project and above all by living on the spot, he learns to see the child in his social setting and to see his learning problems in a wide context.

For most students this is a fairly big gain, a growth in insight and knowledge. If they are students of education, destined to become teachers, the experience has a special value akin to that of the students in the EPA projects described elsewhere in this book. In may encourage or discourage, but at least the vision is a little clearer and the student, if he is eventually to teach in inner city and multiracial schools, a little better prepared. His practical skills are improved, his educational psychology put to the test, his learning theory brought up against the reality. He has necessarily learnt a great deal about teaching and about children's motivation: if he hasn't, then he has had a hard time of it. He has found that to be effective he has had to plan, prepare materials and introduce variety into his work. He has had to set himself clear goals, at the same time being flexible in his demands upon the child. He has had to work out a relationship with the child in which his role has become clear and acceptable to himself and the child – and this is not always easy for a student trying to be companion, friend and tutor all in one. One-to-one teaching is not an easy option, compared with group or class teaching.

The relationship of volunteer to child is also complicated by cultural factors, some of which have to be sorted out in the wider context of the project. It is a fact, for instance, that more women students than men (and more sixth form girls than boys) volunteer for summer projects. From the non-English-speaking immigrant groups, far more boys than girls come to a project; Muslim boys, in particular, are often uneasy with women students as tutors. This situation can result in bad behaviour and refusals to co-operate, and adjustments may have to be made in the arrangements. Related difficulties may arise if students visit Muslim homes. These are obvious examples of cross-cultural difficulties from which a broader understanding of culture in society may arise. More subtly, the same forces operate in many of the activities and in much of the language work throughout the day. Thus, for students of linguistics and social sciences in particular, work on a project can provide a sustained learning experience, one especially that illumines not only that particular area of psycholinguistics which looks at language acquisition and second-language learning, but the sociolinguistic aspects that are, at the present time, receiving greater emphasis in academic studies. Thus, to the student working with immigrant children and living fairly close to the immigrant community, it becomes clear that many of the children's language learning problems relate to social factors rather than purely linguistic ones. The Pakistani child may, with his tutor, practise until he seems to 'know' the areas of English grammar that cause most difficulty (for example, the *s* ending in the present, *My father works* . . . , the past tense verb forms *we went, we played, we saw* . . . , the plural noun endings – *boys, books*) but how will society encourage and reinforce him in his use of these? Hardly at all. At home he will hear either Urdu, or, if the family speaks any English at all, it will probably be a kind of English that lacks the forms the student has been learning, for example, *We go Indian film last night, My two uncle come from Pakistan* – all perfectly intelligible, but unlikely to encourage the child to use the 'correct' forms he has worked away at in class. Cultural attitudes which are different from those of the host community will also be learned at home. Social tradition will inhibit the Pakistani boy from accepting that his sister has as much right to attend the summer project as he has, or from co-operating with her in a play the students may have planned for the morning's work. In time, it will complicate the girl's attitude to the activities too, and to her role in them, and thus what she herself uses language for and how she uses it.

It is clear that for the language and education students who have so far worked on summer projects there is great value in this kind of learning: some opportunities are recognised, some are necessarily missed. The projects we have experience of have recruited students from any and every discipline and dwelt perhaps too fleetingly on the relevance of the project to the students' own studies. A more deliberate planning of recruitment and preparation could very easily build on these links. Preparations within term time, visits to the areas where the project is held, the attachment of students to schools for a term and then their continuous contact with one or two children for the period of the summer project would give them a corpus of data and observations that would add a new dimension to their theoretical studies. The same sort of local link and contact with a backward reader would provide a parallel experience for education students or for language students with a special interest in literacy.

But colleges and university departments have hardly as yet explored the possibility of linking summer project work more formally with the curriculum. It could be a very real possibility provided time is given to its preparation and provided academic staff are willing to work in the schools in term time and on the project itself in the vacation.

CO-OPERATIVE LEARNING

We do not feel that the development of summer project work along these lines would mean that projects lost what till now have been their essential characteristics, notably the goodwill and co-operation of the volunteers. Moreover, if we look again at their conventional mode of operation, we feel that there is something in this which contributes in a very basic way to the curriculum of students but which has not received the recognition it deserves. First, let us think of the very different groups of people and organisations who come together in summer projects. College students predominate, but the help of local sixth formers has already been mentioned; in some cases younger secondary school children have helped, working with juniors and setting up a crèche for under-fives. Immigrant fifth and sixth formers have also made a contribution, a most significant one in that too often the immigrant or minority-group child is forced into the role of receiver or learner; young police cadets and apprentices have also helped. Older professional personnel include teachers and headteachers, college and university staff, youth workers, police, education officers and adults from organisations, community relations councils, etc. Opportunities are created for people to work together in very different ways, in circumstances in which there is respect for the different kinds of expertise they bring and where learning and teaching are closely intertwined. This offers a fruitful experience for all concerned and – if this is not too idealistic – a glimpse of that total learning environment of which Hugh Anderson wrote:

'Education is more than the acquisition of facts: it is the process of learning how to live and an integral part of learning how to live is learning how to give. The problems of overcrowded schools and classes could be perceptibly eased if this principle were to be vigorously applied. Backward children throughout the school – but especially in lower classes – could be helped by their more advanced contemporaries and by senior pupils. *In this way, part of everyone's school experience would be the opportunity to teach a younger or more backward pupil anything from simple mathematics to domestic science.* . . . The whole structure of school could become orientated around this relationship. This is, of course, no alternative to trained, adult professional teaching – but it could, with adequate supervision, prove a most valuable advantage both for the tutor and the tutee. Indeed, the very barrier between tutor and tutee would become broken down and the learning process would be seen for what it is – an integral totality.' (Green and Anderson, 1970;[1] our italics.)

This challenging conception has had too little discussion in our national debate on the education of minorities, or indeed in the education of students – where we should see it as most relevant. It leads us to think that one of the aspects of our school system that might be changed in the 1970s is the way in which we seal off each year group from the one below and teach each year in isolation from all others. The single exception to this is in enlightened infant schools which practise 'vertical grouping' of the fives to sevens. Elsewhere the system of horizontal, hermetically sealed bands ensures that no age group has a model of interests or performance other than that of its contemporaries. Admittedly there are dangers in children identifying with older models of the wrong kind but is this any reason for not presenting constructive models which will challenge individuals to move beyond the peer group common denominator?

In language learning, the role of the older informant is crucial. Young children, acquiring their language and with it, in Edward Sapir's phrase, their 'world view', need above everything else an adult whom they can call their own, with whom to conduct the dialogue that is essential to the acquisition of language. The role of such dialogue between parent and child has been brilliantly shown in the studies of Roger Brown and his associates at Harvard. How crucial it is for the child's 'learning ability' has been studied by the Moscow school of psycholinguists. L. S. Vygotsky was the first to draw attention to the necessity of this early dialogue with an adult for the later development of the 'internalised dialogue' that, he claimed, every individual 'plays over' to himself as an essential accompaniment to thought (Vygotsky, 1962[7]). The dialogue and hence the ability to learn depends on the building during the critical period for language learning of a confident, undisturbed relationship with an adult who has the time, energy and interest to sustain his or her demanding role. This applies to all children acquiring language, regardless of racial or social background, but obviously children in the typical EPA home or children from an immigrant background, whose own parents cannot share with them the language and concepts met in school, are especially at risk. It is for them that the provision of an adult's time, all to themselves, with no other claims competing, is vital. This is the privilege that the middle-class child in the small family has enjoyed during the all important five years before school age.

If this is true of EPA children acquiring English, it is true *a fortiori* of immigrant children. The immigrant child faces the daunting hurdle of a cultural and often religious gulf between his family and his school. He is faced with abrupt adjustment to new behaviour patterns, to new attitudes, to different personal relationships, including sexual relationships and child-parent or child-teacher relationships, to unaccustomed dress and diet. On top of all this, he has to acquire a new language quickly and through it the concepts associated with the school learning situation. He, more than most children, needs Vygotsky's dialogue with a sympathetic adult. Moreover it is not only the young immigrant at infant or junior school level who requires this opportunity for dialogue. The older the immigrant child is when he enters the school, the more urgent is the language problem and the greater the need therefore for the individual dialogue which is the key to language acquisition. Of course, this dialogue does not have to be with a trained teacher.

The affectionate mother, given time, energy and a fair education, manages quite well. So could the teachers' aide with the requisite training.

Some way must eventually be found to provide adult time for those children who in this respect are disadvantaged, and the only realistic solution would be a staffing ratio of teachers to pupils in nursery and primary schools in Educational Priority Areas of something approaching one to one. Obviously this is unrealistic if we think only of trained teachers, and the intelligent use of aides must be seen as part of the answer. Yet the Plowden proposals for the use of aides, modest as they were, have so far proved unacceptable. It is partly for this reason, and as a second-best solution pending the outcome of Halsey's feasibility studies,[2] that we turn attention to summer holiday enrichment and language programmes.

Any honest attempt to face this challenge must lead us back to the question of where the aides in sufficient number are to come from. One source may well lie in the student and sixth-form population. We conclude this chapter with a passage from the editorial in a recent number of the *London Educational Review*[5] in which this theme is developed:

'Perhaps we need a new conception of education as a dual process involving both learning and sharing what is learnt. The model would be not of a school and further education course as a race to the tape with prizes to the swift and marks deducted if you look round (or help) your fellow competitors, but as a rock climb. In this learning model the team is roped together. Each member (student) has *two* obligations, both equally important: to make his own pitch, but immediately to secure the rope and help some other learner up. This could mean sixth formers taking time off from private study to act as 'group leaders' with junior classes, especially in mother tongue or foreign language learning. (An interesting experiment on these lines is being carried on in some twenty schools at the Language Teaching Centre, York.) It could mean students accepting, as a normal concomitant of the privilege of spending three or more years in their personal or professional education, the obligation to spend some time in homes, *à la* Gina Armstrong [that is, as home visitors to mothers with young children], or as teachers' aides in nursery and primary school, or sitting beside and *learning with* the 'reluctant learner' aged 15 plus' (Hannam *et al.*, 1971[3]).

'Are we ready to accept all the implications . . . of such a model? Or are we too deep in our educational rut to break out and try to behave as if we were truly members of a community rather than competitors in a hen run?'

This is undoubtedly a challenge to the student and sixth form population, as much as it is to their teachers and to the teachers who must accept them as allies. Perhaps it is in offering even brief glimpses of the possibilities of the 'rock-climbing' model of education that the summer project movement will prove most valuable.

REFERENCES

1   Jean Green and H. Anderson, *Youth Tutors Youth*, Community Service Volunteers, 1970.
2   A. H. Halsey (ed), *Educational Priority. EPA Problems and Policies*, vol 1, HMSO, 1972.
3   C. Hannam *et al.*, *Young Teachers and Reluctant Learners*, Penguin, 1971.
4   E. Hawkins (ed), *A Time for Growing. A Handbook for Organisers of Summer Projects*, Community Relations Commission, 1971.
5   *London Educational Review*, ('The Education of Minorities'), vol 2, no. 1, University of London Institute of Education, 1973.
6   H. E. R. Townsend, *Immigrant Pupils in England. The LEA Response*, NFER, 1971, (Ch 7, 'Summer holiday projects' by E. M. Brittan).
7   L. S. Vygotsky, *Thought and Language*, MIT Press, 1962.

Chapter Ten

Community Action in Liberal Studies

BY DAVID BROCKINGTON

David Brockington is lecturer in Social Work at Bristol Polytechnic. He was educated at a polytechnic and at York University where he studied Philosophy. In 1970 he began research at Bristol University into 'alternative' teaching methods and learning possibilities, and the same year started part-time lecturing at Bristol Polytechnic.

I would like to explain in what follows how I came to be convinced of the educational and social efficacy and necessity of integrating work in the community into the curriculum, both in higher and in secondary education; to describe how I have tried to go about this; and to relate some of the inherent educational and social considerations and the effects of community action projects upon the students and upon those whom we have sought to understand and become involved with.

The first class I ever had to teach as a lecturer in liberal studies at Bristol Polytechnic, then Brunel Technical College, two and a half years ago, beginning innocent and green as a cabbage, took place on a Friday evening for two hours, from seven to nine at night, with a group of HNC day release medical laboratory students whose study day had already lasted ten hours and with whom, for their remaining two hours, I was expected to relate, stimulate, and provide the broader based educational perspectives intimated by the DES circular in its recommendation of humanities subjects for all science and technology students.

I thought then, and still do now, that the situation was absurd if not immoral. Nothing more illiberal could have been contrived. No one wanted to be in that room; they didn't want to be there, tired and exhausted at the butt end of the day and of the week;

I didn't want to be there, compelled by ridiculous timetabling into forcing them to listen to my material when their desires pulled towards relaxing talk in a pub, and their minds towards sleep. I soon abandoned that time spot with that group and instead made visits to theatres and cinemas at other points throughout the week and tried to introduce ideas and discussions over drinks around the productions we saw.

But that was just the beginning of a feeling I had experienced, which developed into a certainty, that so-called liberal studies was, and was felt by students to be, mostly a waste of time and at best a 'scive', despite all the efforts of their liberalisers. I was being continually confronted with groups for liberal studies periods who threw up for me many insights into teaching and learning problems which have been both practical and philosophical. How was I to communicate with day release students from industry who felt indifference and even animosity to the idea of 'liberal studies'; students who justified to themselves sitting in a classroom and being where they were on an entirely utilitarian ground – better job status and more money, and with whom, because of this particular justificatory educational outlook, I had no social contract. With those who taught them their vocational subjects they had some contact; but I had to forge a relationship on other grounds. How does education differ from vocation training or from socialisation? What did it mean to have authority as a teacher? On what other basis, if any, could I be morally justified in exercising authority, if I had no consensus of interest from those I was trying to teach?

Concurrently with all this, I was doing an M.Ed. research degree at Bristol University and living in a city which made me question more and more the quality of urban life and of education: a city whose conservatism and affluent indifference was making me more and more angry. It was at this time that I met David Gordon, a teacher at Brunel Technical College working also with the humanities department, whose teaching methods I have tried to emulate and to develop since they seemed to me to provide the germs of answers to many of the teaching problems I was faced with. David Gordon had in large part abandoned the suffocating unreality of the classroom with groups of bakers, printers, builders and plumbers, to take them out into the twilight city with its housing problems and social and racial conflicts, described for us by sociologists, to meet at a grassroots level the people with the problems. Because he had arrived at this Bristol Polytechnic humanities department before

Brunel College was hived off as a separate entity, he had been involved with groups 'right across the board'. The first major project with these mixed groups was during rag week 1970, when a 'stakhanovite' exercise led to the clearance of a waste site and the creation of an adventure playground. From there, the same groups or their successors have come under the umbrella of the joint students' union, still involving the printer as much as the town planner. It was with these groups that he rebuilt Bristol's first adventure playground, supporting it until it was established and thriving. This experience enabled him to pilot the scheme at the children's hospital and it was at this point that the two of us developed complementary roles in community action. With these groups of student workers, he was the driving force behind the building of the first adventure playgrounds for children in the deprived areas of Bristol.

What I was gleaning from my research, what I was learning about the city from living in it, and what David Gordon was practising in his teaching identified for me the objectives I soon proposed and intended to fulfil in my own community action projects.

Firstly, I was sure that I could not teach anything to any student until I had established an area of common interest and that the only way in which I could gain any teaching influence was in a consensus contractual situation. Secondly, I was becoming increasingly convinced that none of our social science disciplines is useful as an armchair exercise alone, and that the best way to understand moot social problems is through personal involvement with them and in them. (I think that this is a fairly sound empirical observation, though some of our critics seem to have lost sight of it.) People learn the ropes by climbing them, not by talking about climbing them or viewing them from a distance likely to produce distortion rather than objectivity. And since I am as much concerned to socialise into a disposition as well as to disseminate information, I must be mindful of teaching 'how' as well as providing the facts. (See Gilbert Ryle's *The Concept of Mind*, 1949, chapter 1, on the distinctions between 'knowing how' and 'knowing that'.)

I am certain that a large part of what makes education seem separate in the clinical or ivory tower sense from 'real life', is that it is. I am also convinced that we can no longer afford, if indeed we ever could, to educate people who have information but who do not and/or cannot act upon it. It has been suggested in a recently published Penguin Education Special, *Television and the People* by

Brian Groombridge, 1972, that the purveying of more and more information and data does not in itself generate acts of social responsibility through heightened awareness, because the recipients of that information are not thereby offered a ticket into any arena of power and influence (cf. the ecology debate). This correlates, I think, very closely to the situation of the teacher and the learner. Data on their own will frustrate. We must not be traduced by words. Education can transform as well as transmit culture and we are only beginning to realise that that is what education as an agency must do. I think that we have to resist in the structure of education – in the physical institutions and in content and in teaching methods – the tendency towards a distancing process from the community, from involvement in its problems and thus from the methodological significance of utilisation of the reality of familiar and immediate social problems as vehicles into an understanding of more abstract areas of theory and conceptualisation. Nuffield science has been about this.

One of my basic objectives revolves around this attempt to use 'real life' situations (and I realise that that is ontologically loaded) as optimum learning contexts for the students to more readily and easily find their way into more rarefied theoretics. (I try to construct in my courses the same sort of learning situations as a science teacher would construct in his laboratory, except that my variable factors are people's and personalities' needs and conflicts as well as the students themselves.) Many of our students from a technical or scientific background have difficulty in understanding other areas of conceptualisation. I would contend in this respect that what Basil Bernstein (1961) has had to say concerning differential language codes between social classes and the bearing this has on educational achievement is as relevant to science and technology students in further education as it is to the secondary school child. (See *Education Economy and Society: A Reader in the Sociology of Education*, Free Press, 1961, Basil Bernstein 'Social Class and Linguistic Development; a theory of Social Learning'.) If this is the case, then it would be arrogant and insensitive of us as teachers to plod on and on through the illuminations of sociology psychology and social psychology in an evangelical belief that the profundity of the insights could not forever remain unapparent. I think that they quite easily can and even if we do succeed in transmitting the data, that alone, as I have said, would be useless and frustrating. You can teach people to understand intellectually that, for instance, there exist intolerable conditions in mental hospitals. But that is not enough either educationally or democratically. I want all the 'knowing that' to be the basis of changes in attitude and of action. You can know that something is the case quite nonchalantly and clinically; but this is not adequate when we are faced as a race with societal problems that demand more of us than recognition of the facts. Recognition is the first step only – we must also act upon what we know. The importance of action is not just centred around the possibility of change but is important in the sense of the creativeness of personal involvement.

What led me to the construction of an adventure playground for the Bristol Children's Hospital psychiatric unit was in part, at least, an initial desire to teach some aspects of the psychology of aggression to a group of mechanical engineers. As I have intimated, my problem as a teacher was how, most effectively, to teach what I wanted to teach and how, more fundamentally, I should best construct a relationship with the group as a prerequisite for teaching anything.

I found that in building the playground where we were all meeting and relating to some very disturbed children, questions as to the nature and cause of their often very aggressive behaviour arose naturally out of that context. Questions began to be asked to which I could give no adequate answers and so I arranged talks on psychosis and emotional disturbance with a consultant psychiatrist eager to help, which in the classroom and without direct experience of the children would have been topics of little connection or significance to the students' lives or terms of reference. In part, what was happening in the teaching sense was the provision of ostensive definition. It was also to do with the principle of situational involvement as opposed to passive acts of listening and jotting down in mind or on paper. Within a week, my relationship with the group had changed: they were enthusiastic and on first name terms with me and some were offering to help at week-ends and in the evenings in the collection of materials and other chores.

The Children's Hospital psychiatric unit (see P. E. Copus and W. Lumsden Walker; The Psychiatric Ward in a Children's Hospital: A Review of the First Two Years. Reprinted from *The British Journal of Psychiatry*, volume 121, number 562, September 1972), at the time of my arrival in October 1971, was dealing with twelve day patients, four and sometimes five of whom slept on the ward at night during weekdays. The unit was closed at weekends. The twelve children and the five or six nursing staff were contained within two main rooms, a thirty foot corridor and shared two other rooms used mostly by the occupational and the physio-therapists, next to which was a small night-nurses consulting room and a minute kitchen to service the ward.

I was told by the nurses that the atmosphere on the ward, simply as a product of the lack of space, quite often became intolerable. No outdoor facility had been provided for the unit, and to take the children out to get some air meant walking them around the streets. My brief was clear: to provide some play facilities in the hospital garden, in an attempt to offer some outlet for energy, and embodying the opportunities to explore, climb, slide and hide away alone, if need be, from adults or with adults in a situation less structured than on the ward. The hospital garden was, in fact, a beautiful potential setting with five trees (we have learnt that if you don't have trees on a playground site, then you have to build trees – which is a ridiculous occupation and quite hard) which gave ample opportunity for the students, the children and myself to live out all our Robinson Crusoe fantasies in the building of platforms and tree houses, accessible by rope nets and from ladders. It was important that the children were involved in the building of their playground and that is true as a sort of blueprint axiom for all our projects. It is no good at all going into a situation with a do-gooding sense of patronage. The process is one of self-help, with the students providing support.

We built a playground from nothing and quickly, as has always been the necessity, although in this instance there was just enough money to purchase round timber from the Forestry Commission instead of using the scrap splintery wood scrounged from demolition sites, which characterises the materials used in the city adventure playgrounds. David Gordon's students began by providing timber for the tower as a course exercise: a group of his sea cadets erected the much used aerial runway, rope ladders and other rope work. When he handed over to me, I was in a position to slow the pace deliberately in order to involve my students in greater depth in the project.

I judged the situation on the unit to be of emergency proportions in terms of the psychological stress caused by the geographical structure and smallness of the ward. If this was to be a therapeutic unit in which children were taken out of stress situations at home or at school or from elsewhere, then the physical environment was,

I believed, of as much importance as any other feature of their treatment and indeed would be likely to affect it. So we built quickly, but not too quickly, because I also believed that a large part of the importance of being at the place, doing the project, both for the hospital nursing staff and the students, was in getting to know the kids. (I am not now so convinced of the efficacy of exposure to the students from the children's point of view, since a case could be made out that the exposure to a large number of people was overdemanding on the 'disturbed' child and not at all therapeutic. However, this consideration has not come about from any effects I ever perceived of the relationship between my students and the children, but rather from my perception of the day-to-day exposure of the children to large numbers of hospital staff who were not and could not be regarded by the children as 'outsiders' as could my students, but who were involved in the structure of the ward as non-neutral agents. Because no child ever had to come out to play, my students were in fact neutral in the sense of being non-impinging personalities in the child's life on the ward.)

We built what could have been built in six weeks in just under six months, gently getting to know the children. A circuit of tree houses joined by walkways of rope and timber, aerial runways, nets and rope ladders encircled a wooden fortress with a tower.

I think the best testimony to the success of the physical project, and the enthusiasm and hard work of the students, emerged when children came on a visit from a school for the mentally subnormal, some of them very physically feeble and uncoordinated and played, climbed and tested themselves out on the structures. It was one mongol boy of twelve who was the first of all the children to exploit the highest of the platform access points into the tallest tree and come down alive, perhaps as a result of the tremulous prayers of his teacher onlookers. After only half-an-hour, those teachers were convinced that we should come to their school to engage in a project for them and told me that they had seen in the space of their visit more physical and creative development in their children than they had seen during the whole of the school year. Children from the unit itself, at first 'truanting' from the hospital, were tending to run away only to play in the garden.

But, throughout the project, I had to fight indifference and opposition from many sources: from my own department who regarded the work I was doing with the students as mere entertainment (I hoped that what I was doing would be at least entertaining); from the students' parent department who really wanted me to be teaching industrial sociology (I rejoined that I would be very prepared to outline the correlations between industrial development and ecological collapse) and were worried about what employers might think and about how I was anyway going to assess their students; and finally from the hospital works department and administrators who, after three months of use in the summer by increasing numbers of satisfied children and visiting parents, closed the playground because it was thought to be dangerous, perhaps by its very 'adventure' nature. That closure decision was taken without anyone having consulted me or any of those involved and without any engineer having observed any child play on any of the structures. At that point, six months of ingenuity and hard work and over three thousand hours of involvement and commitment were deflated and collapsed.

Not much of an achievement in communication or 'community' terms. Basically, the criticisms concerning our building techniques and materials were, I would argue, trivial; and such defects as did exist could have been corrected within a week. The playground remained closed for ten months. In fact, the situation has now been retrieved and is well on the way to a satisfactory resolution with the hospital works department having helped with rebuilding and much more expensive materials, and having entered into the sort of working relationship which we had wanted from the outset and had not achieved.

At Farleigh Mental Hospital, just after the notorious trials in 1970 in which nurses were accused and some subsequently jailed for violence towards patients, students determined to discover and to help the situation if they could. An outdoor adventure playground on which some of the high dependency patients began with encouragement and support to climb and explore, led to our major Farleigh project. (See *The Guardian*, Special Feature, 9 June 1972.) During the last two years, over 10,000 hours of commitment later, and nearly 2,500 student helpers passing through and compounding the asset of the process of exposure to new forces and new ideas, a facility – an indoor adventure playroom – unique in the hospitals of this country, has emerged out of the resolution and strength of student imagination and labour.

In many ways, the Farleigh Hospital project represents the high point of my association with Dave Gordon in community action. Student concern led to the demand for expertise imported from other projects: the outdoor playground was seen as a pilot scheme of sufficient value to convince the Hospital Board that it should invest money in a facility of the highest quality. This enabled Dave Gordon as organiser to sell the idea of a full year's course involvement for Dip.A.D. construction students at the art college. We now have money, craftsmanship and professional guidance. To this combination, we added between us the vast labour force of volunteers. Now that the indoor scheme is completed (the pioneering stage) we have the opportunity, for the first time in any project, to observe and record the long-term effects of our involvement. The Farleigh project is of national importance, not because it is a perfect scheme, but because it raises hopes and provides some useful guidance for other, similar institutions.

Not one of us involved believes, though, that any laurels are to be rested on, or that anything like final solutions have been found. In fact now, the very existence of the playroom proposes that there are other roles for the mental subnormal nursing staff to fulfil, apart from the purely custodial; and in that that recognition may well produce conflicts for those people so undernourished over the years in terms of NHS capital resource, then it is and will be our job to continue our support and involvement in and with their problems.

We have climbed an Everest of difficulties from many sources – the local authority apropos the city adventure playgrounds; the respective institutional management networks apropos the hospital projects; the education machine of our own employers; heads of departments demanding principles of assessment; the dreary speculation as to insurance coverage for any student leaving the Polytechnic campus. It has all been very negative (although, since we are conflict theorists, we believe not dysfunctional), and without exception although the problems that each critic raises are different, each misses the fundamental point and objective in what we do.

Let me take the example of the educational assessment objection to highlight the misunderstanding, and consider the following questions. How, at Farleigh, would one assess the effect of the recognition that Richard, an athetoid spastic with desperate speech problems, is in fact a person? How, at the children's hospital, should I assess the implications and ramifications of the growth of delicate and subtle handling of children or of the effect of compassionate humour emerging in play? Or of the forging of new friendships with the children and of guidance, teaching and leadership roles?

Of course, I could fill in on my register sheets which ask for class content details 'Learnt that Richard was a person today, etc.'. But that would be an act of violence to what was happening. And, of course, I do not deny that there are methods, sophisticated and otherwise, of assessing attitude or cognitive or personality developments. What I am saying is that to have posed the question in the first place, to have viewed the situations as appropriate to that type of assessment approach is to have misunderstood the significance of an essential form/content distinction in education.

What I mean is this: I said before that I was not interested in merely teaching data, teaching that something is the case; and I said that I wanted the 'knowing that' to be the basis of action and involvement. And here is the nub of it: you can teach people to understand (intellectually) the concepts of sympathy and compassion, just as you can teach them the components x, y and z of a problem. But what I want to socialise students into is something much more than just an academic understanding of a problem. I want to present persons with the possibility of exercising their understanding in a much wider sense; to present them with the opportunity, for some perhaps the first in their lives beyond the immediate family unit, to engage as a matter of course (in this case a liberal studies course) in a *process of care*.

In short, I'm saying that it is not possible to teach things like tolerance and sympathy and compassion for others – and those are the things it looks as though we must teach if we are to survive – just by teaching what those concepts mean (witness the failure of a great deal of religious education).

What I think you have to do, if you ever want more than just academic understanding, is to demonstrate those virtues by practising them yourself and by yourself constructing and insinuating people into situations where they can practise and emulate those demonstrations, and where they may come to regard those activities as a natural part of their education and of their lives.

To assess any of these developments would be to assess a quality of life, of life styles and of attitudes in the very long term. To try to quantify in the short term, to ask what a student did this morning or what he learnt this morning is to ask too much of a short-term context-type question which can only be adequately answered by rejecting the question in favour of other form and process perspectives of life education.

We all of us live, and I'm sorry if what I say sounds hackneyed but that forms part of our problem, in a world of terrifying destruction, physical, psychological, ecological; with a nuclear sword of Damocles hovering above our heads; with the threat of hopeless violence constantly with us. In such a world, my department at the Polytechnic wishes to develop an academic humanities degree with all the traditions of content and teaching which that will surely involve. In Londonderry and in Bogside, children living in a community in an advanced state of collapse are being taught Latin and medieval history in their 'learning rooms' by their educators. Well I want none of that, or very little of what that means in terms of the acceptance of educational and life priorities. What I want to try to do is to help socialise persons in their community and *also* their community into caring involvement with others and with each other.

SUMMARY

I have made several claims for community action projects.

Firstly, I have said that they are instrumental as teaching *methods*. In my experience they have provided the consensus of interest required for the social contract of the teaching function in further education.

Secondly, I believe that they can provide optimum learning situations for understanding what might otherwise be regarded as boring and thus prove inaccessible. For instance, I maintain that I could construct an 'O' level, and particularly a mode 3 CSE literature syllabus around an adventure playground project with its congruent extensions into role play and dramatic play and movement. In fact, I have used the projects as raw material for other syllabus requirements where community action as such could not, for whatever particular reasons, be fitted in, using the contacts and situations for the development of communication skills, with students interviewing staff and patients; using videotapes and cameras and recorders to produce programmes. I have taught philosophy in the Farleigh setting. Asking 'What is a person?' and taking students through the conceptual crevasses of Strawsonian theory (see: P. F. Strawson, *Individuals*, Methuen, 1964) or posing ethical questions as to the justification of behaviour: should we euthenase? I have not yet looked much to literature for insights into the dilemma of the sick, nor yet produced a play with students and patients. Nor have I really looked to Talcott Parsons for a detailed understanding of institutional structure or to the insights of R. D. Laing. But these are to come I hope.

Thirdly, I believe that community action projects provide an entrée into action and democratic participation on the basis of understanding such that what is understood does not frustrate by being *merely* understood.

And fourthly, and most significantly, such projects provide the opportunity for establishing networks and patterns of sympathetic and sensitive behaviour in and through involvement.

CONCLUSION

Teaching liberal studies, I have been in contact with young workers whose departments really wanted me to teach them remedial English so that they might apply to employers in grammatical letters of application for non-existent jobs. Printers are a good example of this. To have taken them out into the city and onto the four adventure playgrounds which now exist and have in fact been largely built by such groups, is seen by some to be almost subversive and counter-productive to their needs. It is neither. John Dewey in *Democracy and Education* observed 'When educators conceive vocational guidance as something which leads up to a definitive, irretrievable and complete choice both education and the chosen vocation are likely to be rigid, hampering further growth.'

This description fits without dissonance the liberal studies under the guise of 'complementary studies' which is really pure vocation extension and is what occurs now.

A strong case could be made out, at this stage of our industrial and social development, that to take students out onto the hills to enjoy and learn to ride a horse, was just as liberating an experience as developing literacy or numeracy. And that is a cultural and political observation.

As far as I am concerned, I win the educational and social battle when I hear from a student his speculation, after working hard at building a tree house at a playground, that he as a mechanical engineer could find his way into forestry as a life and as a livelihood.

Perhaps we finally win the liberal studies battle when liberal studies as such is made redundant and when the vocation disciplines are themselves taught and conducted liberally and not in the constricting and cramping way we have to cope with and tolerate at this moment.

As I have issued the warning not to be traduced by words, so do not be.

I have tried to give some short account of what we are about down here in Bristol but what I have said has not been undeliberatively sketchy; quite the contrary, for I hope that if you have any thought that what I describe may be exciting or controversial, meaningful or wrong-headed, then please don't just think that but come and see what we are doing.

Index